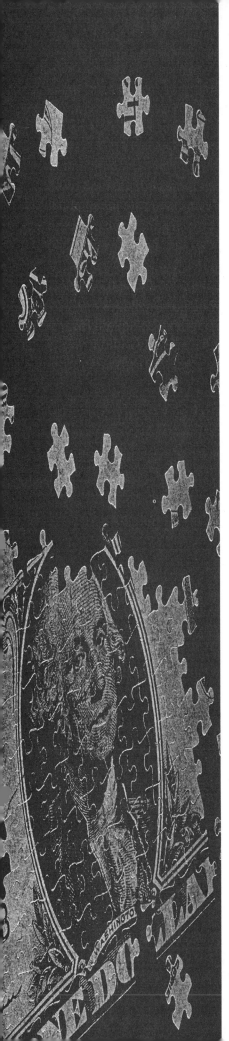

Becoming
Money Wise

Biblical and Practical Principles
Encouraging Faithful Management
of God's Money

Ronald J. Chewning, CFP
Illustrated by Winston T. Pear

SAINT LOUIS

1 2 3 4 5 6 7 8 9 10   07 06 05 04 03 02 01 00 99 98

Acknowledgements

I have been blessed to have so many wonderful people assist me in making this book a reality. Without the assistance and guidance of others, this book would not have been possible.

My sincere thanks to the following:

Phyllis Chewning, my wife, who gave so much of her time to both edit and offer insightful suggestions. Her constant encouragement and support helped in the writing of this book.

Linda Leinhos, my secretary, who spent many hours typing and organizing the material. Her patience with the constant changes and her interest in completing this book were invaluable. Special thanks to Linda's husband, James, who provided needed technical support.

Winston Pear, the book's illustrator, who did such a masterful job with the drawings of Financial Freddie.

Rev. Larry Reinhardt, LCMS Director of Stewardship, who was instrumental in promoting the need for a book such as this.

Fred Gerds, Karen Eggemeyer, and my brother, Richard Chewning, for their editing support.

Rev. David Belasic, Rev. Donald Burch, Steve Cecchetti, Richard Johnson, Kirk Mattes, and Pam Moksness for their valuable suggestions.

Rev. Ray Scherbarth and Rev. Ronald Young, my pastors, for their ongoing encouragement.

Contents

Preface

Although money is an integral part of our lives, many of us, regardless of age, sex, race, or background, lack a proper understanding of it. We may believe the only money problem we face is not having enough. More than likely, however, we have an adequate amount but need to use it more wisely. Money is good, as are all gifts from God, but because of our sinful state we often use money for wrong and foolish purposes. We can become fixated upon the things of this world and place God into a secondary position. This book will explore how we can properly view money. It all begins by learning what God has to say about this area of our lives, then recognizing His authority over our lives and possessions.

God gives us the freedom to determine how we want to spend money, but the Bible is very clear about what God expects from us. Because we interact with money daily, we have many opportunities to rise to those expectations in our perception and use of money. The fact that God put all things, including money, at our disposal means we have an obligation to use them according to His plan. To do that, we seek His wisdom and understanding.

The Bible has more than 2,000 verses about money and many of Jesus' parables deal with money and possessions. From these, we can see God's instructions and plans regarding money:

"No one can serve two masters. Either he will hate the one and love the other, or he will be devoted to one and despise the other. You can't serve both God and Money" (Matthew 6:24). Our love, desire, and worries about money can consume us. Money and possessions may become so important that God is squeezed out of our lives and without warning, money may become god. When our focus is on Christ, we have a different perspective and use our money for His purposes.

"What good will it be for a man to gain the whole world, yet forfeit his soul?" (Matthew 16:26) True wisdom is found in knowing that happiness is living for Christ. If we gain the world, we find it doesn't bring contentment and peace. All that we need and want comes from our relationship with God.

"But seek His Kingdom, and these things will be given to you as well" (Luke 12:31). God wants our love and commitment and, as our loving Father, He will provide for and bless us. Seeking Him makes everything else happen.

"For the love of money is a root of all kinds of evil" (1 Timothy 6:10). Money is not evil, but the love of it is. God speaks against improper priorities and attitudes regardless of whether we are rich or poor.

"Watch out! Be on your guard against all kinds of greed; a man's life does not consist in the abundance of his possessions" (Luke 12:15). If we are not careful, we get caught up lusting after more money and possessions. But God has a plan and will provide for our needs.

This book uses these and other verses, as well as counsel from other authors, to share God's wisdom and instruction so we can become more productive and faithful with money.

Money skills generally don't come naturally but are acquired by reading and studying. I wish you well on your journey to become money wise. God's blessings to you as together we serve Christ with our lives and money.

Ronald J. Chewning

Hello! I'm Financial Freddie. Together we will learn both biblical and practical money principles on saving, planning, spending, investing, giving, and budgeting. Let's get started!

Chapter 1

Faithful Stewardship

> It is fitting that we begin with a discussion about God's ownership of both our lives and our resources. We are to use God's gifts for His purposes.

Give, and it will be given to you. A good measure, pressed down,
shaken together and running over.
Luke 6:38

Far too often, we understand "stewardship" to be that yearly church program everyone must endure. But stewardship is *everything* we do as disciples of Christ. We live out our faith as we respond to God's call to be faithful with all His blessings. Stewardship involves our entire lives.

This book focuses on the stewardship of God's money, but stewardship encompasses much more than how we manage or share that money. Stewardship is more than giving a few hours to church or the needy; it is more than using our energy and talents to help others. Stewardship is what we do with *all* that God gives us. Stewardship is our response to God's love for us. We first give ourselves before we can give our time, energy, ability, and money. Stewardship is "heart" work.

Carl W. Berner, Sr., in his book *The Power of Pure Stewardship* quotes a Sunday school child who was asked to explain stewardship: "Stewardship means that life is like a great ship loaded with cargo to be delivered to many people in many places. God is the owner of the ship and its cargo, but He has made me the captain."[1] God has given us cargos of life, time, energy, talents, money, intelligence, and ability to work. Our job is to use them according to His will.

Stewards as Servants

In Scripture, the steward is depicted as a person who manages another person's belongings. The steward *represents* the owner. The steward is a caretaker, custodian, chosen servant, an important person in a privileged, responsible position. "Now it is required that those who have been given a trust must prove faithful" (1 Corinthians 4:2). Every believer is a steward because God has given us time, abilities, and possessions and, as His representatives, we are responsible for the resources He entrusts to us.

As Christian stewards, we see our whole lives as opportunities to serve Christ. Every decision, position, and activity is part of our stewardship. The Holy Spirit enables us to be faithful stewards.

We might compare our role as stewards to a banker. When we deposit our money in a bank, we expect our banker to manage our investments prudently and to keep them safe. We don't tolerate mismanagement or corruption. We also expect a fair return on our money, as well as courteous treatment. Just as we expect a return from our banker, God wants a return on His investment in us.

As God's "bankers," we are to manage all we have in a God-pleasing way. In the parable of the talents, we learn that He wants our resources to grow and we are to be responsible whether we are given little or much. With bigger blessings comes added responsibility: "From everyone who has been given much, much will be demanded; and from the one who has been entrusted with much, much more will be asked" (Luke 12:48). The Lord expects that we will do a good job. When we put our trust in Him, He will show us His will and will provide us strength to do His work. We have the confidence and ability to move forward because we know the Holy Spirit will guide and assist us. Our mission as stewards is not only to give our time, abilities, and money but to speak the Gospel message of life, hope, and joy to all. We become effective stewards when we live our lives in partnership with Christ.

Purposes for Money

"Be shepherds of God's flock that is under your care, serving as overseers—not because you must, but because you are willing, as God wants you to be; not greedy for money, but eager to serve" (1 Peter 5:2). As shepherd-stewards, we carefully examine our attitudes toward money. We may look at money as a vehicle for security, power, independence, or influence, but the real purpose of money is to live out God's love and power in our lives. Following are four basic purposes for money.

10

Give us this day our daily bread...

1. To Provide Basic Needs—To sustain life, we need food, clothing, and shelter. The apostle Paul assures us that God will provide for our needs. "And my God will meet all your needs according to His glorious riches in Christ Jesus" (Philippians 4:19). We may have little or much, but knowing that God will supply our needs, we become dependent on Him and grateful for His daily provision. God gives out of love and we receive with thankfulness. God's Word teaches us to be content and enjoy what we've been given, "But if we have food and clothing, we will be content with that" (1 Timothy 6:8).

2. To Confirm Direction—God may use our abundance or lack of it to confirm His direction for the many financial decisions we must make. Certainly having or not having the money for a purchase may not reflect God's will, but through money He has the opportunity to get our attention. If we have exhausted every avenue to raise money, God may be telling us that He does not want us to have what we want or that the timing is inappropriate. Only God knows what is best for us. We recognize and accept God's direction. "I know, O LORD, that a man's life is not his own; it is not for man to direct his steps" (Jeremiah 10:23).

Spending money is a daily occurrence. Spending God's money wisely requires faithful obedience. In our prayers we ask for guidance and, if need be, patience. "Guide me in Your truth and teach me, for You are God my Savior, and my hope is in You all day long" (Psalm 25:5).

3. To Give to Others—A loving heart opens our eyes and pocketbooks to those in need. As people who have received God's grace, we become very generous. "Share with God's people who are in need. Practice hospitality" (Romans 12:13).

Scripture points out the responsibility we have as believers to help those in need. Those with more than enough are to share. In fact, even those with little are exhorted to share out of their poverty. "And do not forget to do good and to share with others, for with such sacrifices God is pleased" (Hebrews 13:16). God gives freely and generously to us; we are to give God's gifts to others.

4. To Illustrate God's Power—God often uses money to demonstrate His power. When there is a need, God provides a miracle so His will is carried out. We see God's power in action when the unexpected gift of money appears. Even though we are faithless and disobedient, He continually proves His faithfulness to us. "You will be made rich in every way so that you can be generous on every occasion, and through us your generosity will result in thanksgiving to God" (2 Corinthians 9:11).[2]

Transferring Control to God

A man was hanging from a cliff a thousand feet above the ground. He was frightened and screamed, "Is there anyone up there who can help me?" Just then, he heard a booming voice from above that said, "Yes, I will help you. I am the Lord. Just relax and let go." There was a long pause. Then the man said, "Is there anyone else up there who can help me?"

Letting go is never easy. For many of us, relying on ourselves is a difficult habit to break. The challenge is to break the emotional attachment we have to things so we can use what we have for God's service. Transferring control is a faith issue with which we wrestle daily. Our goal is to learn how to give all we have to the Lord and to trust Him to give back all we need. In the book of Malachi, God tells His people that if they faithfully give, He will provide. " 'Test me in this,' says the LORD Almighty, 'and see if I will not throw open the floodgates of heaven and pour out so much blessing that you will not have enough room for it' " (3:10). As we trust in Him, God will show His faithfulness to us.

A Stewardship Attitude

Our attitude toward our money, time, and talents determines our heart for stewardship. The important question is, are we willing to surrender both ourselves and our material gifts to Him? If we don't put our trust in God, we hold on tightly to the blessings He gives us. If we hold fast to what we have and covet even more, we will never experience the joy of giving. Because God loves to give, He replenishes what we give. We may not always receive replacements for material things, but God will surely fill us with blessings money can't buy.

An attitude of generosity is shown in the story of the widow's mite in Luke 21:1–4: "As He looked up, Jesus saw the rich putting their gifts into the temple treasury. He also saw a poor widow put in two very small copper coins. 'I tell you the truth,' He said, 'this poor widow has put in more than all the others. All these people gave their gifts out of their wealth; but she out of her poverty put in all she had to live on.' "

In these verses we see that Jesus watched what people gave. He did not praise the rich who gave large sums, but He rejoiced in the widow's two small copper coins. The widow was blessed because she gave out of her poverty. In Jesus' mind the total collection of the others was less than what the widow gave because the rich gave out of their surplus. Her giving was made possible by her willingness to sacrifice. She gave up something of value, and that is what Jesus praises. Her two coins were less important to her than her desire to please God. The widow possessed a loving and giving heart.

The key is that it's not the amount of what we give that's important, but our attitude toward giving. What are we willing to give up? Are we willing to release something we value? "For where your treasure is, there your heart will be also" (Matthew 6:21). Giving is an expression of one's self. Our giving represents who we are and is an outward expression of an inward grace. In the parable of the Good Samaritan (Luke 10:25–37), three attitudes regarding stewardship are portrayed by the characters in the story.

> On one occasion an expert in the law stood up to test Jesus. "Teacher," he asked, "what must I do to inherit eternal life?"
>
> "What is written in the Law?" He replied. "How do you read it?"
>
> He answered: " 'Love the Lord your God with all your heart and with all your soul and with all your strength and with all your mind;' and, 'Love your neighbor as yourself.' "
>
> "You have answered correctly," Jesus replied. "Do this and you will live."
>
> But he wanted to justify himself, so he asked Jesus, "And who is my neighbor?"
>
> In reply Jesus said: "A man was going down from Jerusalem to Jericho, when he fell into the hands of robbers. They stripped him of his clothes, beat him and went away, leaving him half dead. A priest happened to be going down the same road, and when he saw the man, he passed by on the other side. So too, a Levite, when he came to the place and saw him, passed by on the other side. But a Samaritan, as he traveled, came where the man was; and when he saw him, he took pity on him. He went to him and bandaged his wounds, pouring on oil and wine. Then he put the man on his own donkey, took him to an inn and took care of him. The next day he took out two silver coins and gave them to the innkeeper. 'Look after him,' he said, 'and when I return, I will reimburse you for any extra expense you may have.'
>
> "Which of these three do you think was a neighbor to the man who fell into the hands of robbers?"
>
> The expert in the law replied, "The one who had mercy on him."
>
> Jesus told him, "Go and do likewise."

Attitude 1: *What is yours is mine, and I'm going to take it.*

In the story we see the possessive attitude of the robbers. As thieves they wanted more, and when they saw an opportunity, they took it. Their short-term benefit was at another person's expense. We need to be fearful of possessing such an attitude. We may not plan something as drastic as robbing an individual, a bank, or a store, but we may covet what we don't have or use what we do have improperly. Without recognizing it, we may be robbing God by not honoring Him with our use of His resources. God gave us what we have, and we are responsible for administering those gifts properly. As soon as we start thinking we are the owners, we rob God. By not listening to God as we seek out His plans, we are taking from Him.

Attitude 2: *What is mine is mine, and I'm going to keep it.*

The priest and the Levite on the road to Jericho saw the naked, beaten man but chose not to help. Whatever they were doing that day or their religious constraints were more important than showing compassion. Their roles presupposed their religious background, but they certainly weren't living their faith.

We are likely to struggle more with this attitude than with the first one. We can help the hurting people in our neighborhoods and in the world, but often we choose to close our eyes. Our "keep to ourselves" attitude causes us to be oblivious to the needs of others, and we delude ourselves into believing we are not hurting anybody. We mistakenly go through life believing "What is mine is mine because God gave it to me, and I can do with it what I please." Neither the priest nor the Levite bothered to offer time, assistance, or money. Certainly God has given us all things for our enjoyment, but He desires that our enjoyment consist of being a benefit and blessing to others.

Attitude 3: *What is mine is yours, and I'm going to give it.*

The Samaritan saw the beaten man and took pity upon him. The Samaritan was a stranger, but he was willing to give of his time, ability, and money. We see in the Samaritan a man who felt it was important to use his God-given abilities and time to benefit someone else. He didn't look for repayment or recognition but was willing to serve the man out of care and compassion. The Samaritan didn't just start the healing process for the man but planned to return so he could provide more money if necessary. In essence, he made a pledge. The attitude "what is mine is yours, and I'm going to give it" finds ultimate expression in Jesus, who gave His life so that we might live.

The difference in the characters' responses to the same situation was in their attitudes. The priest and the Levite had the ability but not the right attitude. They chose not to give of their time and ability. They held high positions of authority but chose not to become involved.

Whatever our professions—plumber, secretary, doctor, teacher, or laborer—we need to develop a God-pleasing stewardship attitude that cares about others. Jesus said, "I tell you the truth, whatever you did for one of the least of these brothers of Mine, you did for Me" (Matthew 25:40).

Every society has robbers who misuse and take from others. Fortunately, we also have many good Samaritans who are willing to share their caring and concerned attitudes with others. The good Samaritan put his good intentions into action—this story would never have been told if the good Samaritan only had good intentions. God wants us all to take the time to demonstrate with others the love He's given us.[3]

Responsive Stewardship

Study the following Scripture references to deepen your understanding of biblical stewardship principles. Take notes as you study.

Revere God's ownership of all your property.

Proverbs 3:19 _____

Psalms 24:1 _____

Psalms 50:9–12 _____

Ecclesiastes 5:19 _____

Receive with thankfulness.

    1 Thessalonians 5:18 _____

Regularly give to the Lord.

    Proverbs 3:9–10 _____

    Malachi 3:8 _____

    2 Corinthians 9:7, 11–12 _____

Respond to the needs of others.

    Matthew 25:40 _____

    Proverbs 19:17 _____

    Deuteronomy 15:11 _____

Responsibly use your resources.

    Luke 19:16–17 _____

Reciprocate with your blessings.

    1 Corinthians 16:2 _____

    Proverbs 11:24 _____

    2 Corinthians 8:14 _____

Relinquish your control.

    Deuteronomy 8:17–18 _____

    Galatians 3:3 _____

Rely on the Lord for all your needs.

    Philippians 4:6 _____

    Proverbs 10:3 _____

    Mark 11:24 _____

1 Timothy 6:17 _____

Rejoice that your needs are met.

    Philippians 4:19 _____

    Matthew 6:28–32 _____

    1 Timothy 6:8 _____

Resist the love of money.

    Luke 12:15 _____

    Ezekiel 7:19 _____

    Hebrews 13:5 _____

    Psalms 62:10 _____

    1 Timothy 6:17–18 _____

Resist hoarding.

    Proverbs 11:26 _____

    James 5:3 _____

Remember the Lord's work in your will.

    Proverbs 13:22 _____

    Psalms 49:16–17 _____

    1 Timothy 5:8 _____

We Are Blessed to Be a Blessing

God is the source of all blessings. Stewardship is simply returning to God what He has already given. We truly are a blessed people, and He fills and fulfills our lives so we can be effective and generous stewards. God's plan for our lives is completed when we use our blessings to bless others.

For we are God's workmanship, created in Christ Jesus to do good works. Ephesians 2:10

We are blessed

- In the beginning God **created** the heavens and the earth. Then God said, "Let us make man in our image." Genesis 1:1, 2

- For it is **by grace** you have been saved, through faith—and this not from yourselves, it is the gift of God." Ephesians 2:8

- And those He predestined, He also called; those He **called,** He also justified; those He **justified,** He also **glorified.** Romans 8:30

- For God so loved the world that He gave His one and only Son, that whoever believes in Him shall not perish but have **eternal life**. John 3:16

- And my God will meet **all your needs** according to His glorious riches in Christ Jesus. Philippians 4:19

- Now to Him who is able to do immeasurably more than all we ask or imagine, according to **His power** that is at work within us. Ephesians 3:20

- But we have this **treasure** [Word of God] in jars of clay to show that this all-surpassing power is from God and not from us. 2 Corinthians 4:7

- The goal of this command is **love,** which comes from a **pure heart** and a **good conscience** and a **sincere faith**. 1 Timothy 1:5

- His divine power has given us **everything we need for life and godliness** through our knowledge of Him who **called us** by His own **glory** and **goodness**. 2 Peter 1:3

- If you believe, you will receive **whatever you ask for in prayer**. Matthew 21:22

So that the man of God may be thoroughly equipped for every good work. 2 Timothy 3:17

. . . to be a blessing.

- Jesus replied: "**Love** the Lord your God with **all your heart** and with **all your soul** and with **all your mind**." Matthew 22:37

- A new command I give you: **Love one another.** As **I have loved** you, so you must love one another. John 13:34

- But **love your enemies**, **do good** to them, and **lend** to them without expecting to get anything back. Luke 6:35a.

- Therefore **go and make disciples** of all nations, **baptizing** them in the name of the Father and of the Son and of the Holy Spirit, and **teaching** them to obey everything I have commanded you. Matthew 28:19–20

- I urge you to live a life worthy of the calling you have received. Ephesians 4:1

- Each man **should give** what he has decided in his heart to give, not reluctantly or under compulsion, for God loves a **cheerful giver**. 2 Corinthians 9:7

- You will be made rich in every way so that you can **be generous** on every occasion, and through us your generosity will result in thanksgiving to God. 2 Corinthians 9:11

- **Look after orphans and widows** in their distress. James 1:27b

- This is love for God: **to obey** His commands. 1 John 5:3a

- If a man remains in Me and I in him, he will **bear much fruit** John 15:5

- **Share** with God's people who are in need. **Practice hospitality**. Romans 12:13

(Emphasis added throughout.)

Sharing with someone in need blesses the giver as much as the recipient. We do indeed reap what we sow.

Financial Stewardship

Why do we give? Does God need our gifts? No. God, who created the world, does not need our gifts, but as created and redeemed people of God we have many reasons to give. We are given all things—from a breath of air to the food we eat to a roof over our heads. Even more important, God gave us what we as sinners need most—a Savior. Through Jesus we are brought back into a relationship and partnership with God. "Now if we are children, then we are heirs—heirs of God and co-heirs with Christ" (Romans 8:17).

Our gift of redemption as illustrated in the following story makes our loving and giving possible:

> During the battle of Fredericksburg there was a valley which changed hands a number of times in the course of the day. Toward evening it was dotted with wounded and dying from both sides. In the heat of the day and the dust of battle these men began pleading for water. A young soldier asked permission to take these suffering soldiers some water to drink. But the commanding officer denied him with the words, "You go over that embankment and you too will be shot."
>
> When the cries of the wounded continued, however, and the soldier repeated his request, he finally gave his consent. When this soldier came over the embankment, bucket of water and dipper in hand, and the enemy army realized his purpose, all the firing ceased. It was a beautiful picture—a soldier in gray giving the wounded and dying some water to drink.

> *But when Christ came over the embankment* of heaven to bring the living water to the wounded and dying of this earth, *the firing did not cease.* The church which He came to redeem cast Him out, the government which He had instituted condemned Him to death, and those little people whom He loved so dearly lifted up their wicked hands and voices until they had driven Him out to Calvary for crucifixion. Even then the "firing did not cease." They spat at Him and cried, "If You are the Son of God, come down from the cross."[4]

Christ paid the price for us all through His suffering and death. Our salvation is free because it has been given to us by Jesus' crucifixion and resurrection. "For you know that it was not with ... silver or gold that you were redeemed, ... but with the precious blood of Christ (1 Peter 1:18–19).

From Genesis to Revelation, we see evidence of God's giving. From the beginning chapter of Scripture to the closing Amen, God always gives. God gave Adam the breath of life, and he became a living being. Abraham received the promise that his name would be great and that a great nation would come from him. David ascended to a throne. Solomon obtained great wisdom and insight. As a nation, Israel was given protection and rest. Everything in God's world is in a state of giving: The grass gives, the sun gives, the trees give, the moon gives, the flowers give, the lakes give, the oceans give, the rivers give.

John tells us in his gospel that Jesus gave to those who believed in Him the right to become the children of God (John 1:12). In Galatians, Paul talks about the life lived in the body through faith in the Son of God who loves us and gave Himself for us. Physically and spiritually God holds us in life. If God withdrew His gifts, we would perish.

" 'For in Him we live and move and have our being. As some of your own poets have said, 'We are his offspring' " (Acts 17:28).

The church doesn't use stewardship as a way to take something *from* people. Rather, stewardship is putting into practice God's plan for our lives. It's an investment of our whole life for God.

> Therefore, I urge you, brothers, in view of God's mercy, to offer your bodies as living sacrifices, holy and pleasing to God—this is your spiritual act of worship. Do not conform any longer to the pattern of this world, but be transformed by the renewing of your mind. Then you will be able to test and approve what God's will is—His good, pleasing and perfect will. Romans 12:1–2

God's grace in our lives makes it possible for us first to receive and then to give. There is a story about the highly decorated Mexican War hero, General Sam Houston. Houston was a coarse, belligerent man, but it was said that, after becoming a Christian, he became peaceful and content. "The day came for Sam Houston to be baptized—an incredible event in the eyes of those who knew his previous lifestyle and attitude. After his baptism Houston stated he would like to pay half the local minister's salary. When someone asked him why, his simple response was, 'My pocketbook was baptized too.' "[5]

God's love for Sam Houston and Houston's love for God made giving possible. We give because of God's great and unending love shown to us in the forgiveness of our sins through the sacrifice of Jesus.

How Should We Give?

Giving is a by-product of our faith. Our giving is an outward expression of our priorities and our hearts. If we put God first in our lives, our wallets will be open.

The miracle of stewardship is that the more one gives the more one receives. We don't always receive in kind but what we receive is more precious than what we give because God's gifts to us are greater than our gifts to Him.

Give Firstfruits

"Honor the LORD with your wealth, with the firstfruits of all your crops" (Proverbs 3:9). Since not all of us make a living from agriculture, we don't give of our crops. But the giving principle is the same. The "God first" principle means that we give to God the first portions of our incomes. By doing that, we constantly remember God's ownership. Making our giving a priority confirms the trust that we place in God. We know God will be there for us during the good and bad times, during times of prosperity and times of affliction. Putting God first does not automatically assure us of prosperity. We are called to fit into God's plans, rather than for God to fit into ours. As we are willing to put our lives into God's hands, He blesses us with the peace and joy that comes only from knowing Christ.

One day a farmer came into the house and greeted his wife with a big smile, saying, "I've got some great news. Our finest cow just gave birth to twin calves, one white and one brown. I've got a notion to give one to the Lord and keep one for ourselves."

The wife, being a very perceptive woman, asked, "Which one are you going to give God—the white one or the brown one?"

Her husband replied, "It won't make any difference because we will raise them together and when they are of marketable age, we'll split the proceeds, half for the Lord and half for us."

Well, some time later the farmer entered his house, this time with a very sad look. "I've got some bad news," he said. "The Lord's calf just died."

Without a doubt you will face situations where you could use your money for purposes other than the Lord's. When money gets tight, will you leave out God's offering? Sometimes you absolutely need your money for basic needs; at other times, ask God for strength and wisdom to stay committed to His "God first" principle as you face temptations to put your wants first.

Give Proportionately

Giving proportionately means giving in proportion to the income we receive—not giving a specific dollar amount. "Each one of you should set aside a sum of money in keeping with his income" (1 Corinthians 16:2).

If you earn $100, a tithe (10 percent) would be $10, if you earn $100,000, your proportionate gift would be $10,000. Through God's infinite wisdom and love for us, He makes it possible that a $10 gift is just as important and meaningful as a $10,000 gift. Proportionate giving challenges both the rich and the poor.

Curtis R. Schumacher tells the story of a woman who tried to teach her daughter the meaning of proportionate giving. "She took ten pennies from her daughter's bank and laid them in a row. The mother said, 'These are your ten pennies.' She then put one penny aside and said, 'This is for Jesus.'

The young girl looked at the nine pennies, then at the one. She looked up at her mother, and glancing at the one lonely penny, said, 'Poor Jesus!' "[6] What would the young girl say if she realized that many Christian families actually give less than 10 percent?

Give Sacrificially

A pig and a hen were strolling amicably down the street when they saw a sign at a lunchroom window reading: DELICIOUS HAM AND EGGS.

"Isn't it grand," said the hen, "that together we can give human beings something that delights them?"

The pig frowned. "Yes," he said, "but you're giving out of surplus; for me, giving is a real sacrifice."[7]

From that point of view, most of us have not reached the point of sacrificial giving. At times God asks us to give until we can truly feel the giving. In our giving patterns, some of us will give less than we could, while others will give proportionately, and still others will give sacrificially. "Out of the most severe trial, their overflowing joy and their extreme poverty welled up in rich generosity. For I testify that they gave as much as they were able, and even beyond their ability" (2 Corinthians 8:2–3). Giving sacrificially usually includes one of the following:

- ▸ a rearrangement of priorities
- ▸ a change in lifestyle
- ▸ a forfeiture of something valued

When we give sacrificially, we give our best. It is like having an apple and letting God have the very first bite. As our faith matures, we offer Him more and more choice bites. Sacrificial giving means going into our cupboards—which may be lean already—and finding food for someone in need.

Sacrificial giving is illustrated in 1 Kings 17:7–24: The widow of Zarephath emptied her cupboard for Elijah. Out of obedience and love for God, the widow was willing to give up the last of her bread. Because of her generosity, she and her son survived the famine.

Giving old clothes and other things we don't need or want is not sacrificial giving. Does God bless our convenient, easy giving of loose change? Sacrificial giving is sharing what we would rather keep. When we give something we value, we are giving sacrificially.

Give Regularly

Many of us give an offering each and every Sunday morning out of habit. This approach to regular giving is biblical. "On the first day of every week, each one of you should set aside a sum of money in keeping with his income, saving it up, so that when I come no collections will have to be made" (1 Corinthians 16:2).

If we commit ourselves to giving the firstfruits of our income, our giving becomes regular. In contrast, if we are inclined to give the leftovers each month, we often have nothing left to give, and our giving becomes irregular.

While money may be tight during some periods of time, for the most part, the failure to give is a spiritual problem. It is hard to imagine God accepting the excuses we may conjure up about not honoring Him with our treasures, especially when we read in 2 Corinthians 9:8, "And God is able to make all grace abound to you, so that in all things at all times, having all that you need, you will abound in every good work." God knows our hearts and our motives.

Give Cheerfully

Remember the anticipation and excitement you felt the last time you gave something to someone? "The Lord Jesus Himself said: 'It is more blessed to give than to receive' " (Acts 20:35). Receiving is great, but the exhilaration is greater when we are able to give to or help another person. The Holy Spirit uses our giving to help deepen our faith in Christ. "Each man should give what he has decided in his heart to give, not reluctantly or under compulsion, for God loves a cheerful giver" (2 Corinthians 9:7).

There is a familiar story about the notice in a church bulletin that read, "The Lord loveth a cheerful giver. He also accepteth from a grouch." From Corinthians we understand that we honor God when we cheerfully give from the heart. Giving reluctantly, under compulsion, or from guilt is not pleasing to God. When God established a pattern of giving, it was not to receive gifts from us but to receive us as givers.

Give Quietly

We are proud by nature, so we often have difficulty not wanting credit for extra giving or doing good deeds. Very few of us go up to the highest pinnacle to broadcast our generosity, but we may find small ways to announce our actions. "Be careful not to do your 'acts of righteousness' before men, to be seen by them. It you do, you will have no reward from your Father in heaven" (Matthew 6:1). Certainly some of our acts will be seen by others, but our only purpose is to please God.

> Years ago, *The Chaplain* magazine told how noted preacher Charles Spurgeon and his wife were tabbed as being stingy because they sold all the eggs their chickens laid and wouldn't give any away. Because they always made a profit on their butter, milk, and eggs, rumors circulated that they were greedy.
>
> The Spurgeons, however, endured the criticism graciously, and only after the death of Mrs. Spurgeon was the truth revealed. The records showed that their entire profits had been used to support two needy, elderly widows whose husbands had

spent their lives in Christian ministry.

Our giving may not always be understood, but like the Spurgeons, our responsibility is to give as our heart dictates. What appears on the surface has little significance when our motives are pure.[8]

Tithe

Tithing is the practice of honoring God with one tenth (10 percent) of our income. God is not concerned about the size of the gift, but the motive for it. In Genesis, Abraham gave a tithe to the priest Melchizedek. Jacob vowed to tithe all his income in grateful response to God (Genesis 28:10-22).

> Then Abram gave him a tenth of everything. (Genesis 14:20)

> A tithe of everything from the land, whether grain from the soil or fruit from the trees, belongs to the LORD; it is holy to the LORD. (Leviticus 27:30)

> Will a man rob God? Yet you rob me. But you ask, "How do we rob you?" In tithes and offerings. (Malachi 3:8)

A tithe is giving to God our best, not our leftovers. In the book of Malachi, God chastised the people of Israel because they offered Him their crippled, diseased animals. God is not honored when we give items of no value or as an afterthought.

> "Bring the whole tithe into the storehouse, that there may be food in My house. Test me in this," says the LORD Almighty, "and see if I will not throw open the floodgates of heaven and pour out so much blessing that you will not have room enough for it. I will prevent pests from devouring your crops, and the vines in your fields will not cast their fruit," says the LORD Almighty. Malachi 3:10–11

In the Old Testament the tithe was brought into the storehouse to do the Lord's work. The food was used to feed the priests and their staffs as well as the needy. Still today we bring in our goods and money for the expenses of the church, spreading the Gospel, and helping the needy. Giving God our first and best demonstrates our complete trust and love for Him.

Tithing in the New Testament

In Jesus' time, tithing was both law and tradition. Jesus said nothing to break the law, and He commended those who exceeded the tithe with trusting, loving, cheerful exuberance. Jesus was born a Jew and was taught the Jewish law by devout parents, so we can accept that He was a tither. He came not to break the law but to fulfill it.

Jesus says in Luke 11:42, "Woe to you Pharisees, because you give God a tenth of your mint, rue and all other kinds of garden herbs, but you neglect justice and the love of God. You should have practiced the latter without leaving the former undone." In this verse, Jesus condemns the Pharisees with their laws because their hearts were not right. The Pharisees did a good job with their tithing but failed in their love and care for others. They had an attitude of pride rather than compassion.

Those who argue that the tithe is no longer necessary in the New Testament should take notice of what Jesus asked of the rich young man. Jesus was asking for a much greater commitment than the tithe. "Jesus looked at him and loved him. 'One thing you lack,' He said. 'Go, sell everything you have and give them to the poor, and you will have treasure in heaven. Then come, follow Me'" (Mark 10:21). Because the rich young man put his security in his possessions, Jesus told him to get rid of what he owned. Jesus knew the rich young man's love for his possessions was greater than his love for Jesus. Does Jesus see in us a covetous attitude like the rich young man or a spirit of generosity?

An appropriate question to ask ourselves is "How much of God's money should I keep?" If we believe tithing is still a command or a minimum obligation for us, then we must ask God for His assistance to reach that level of giving. Our tithing can be a benefit in our personal spiritual growth because our lack of giving can be an obstacle to our developing a complete relationship with Christ.

The downside of tithing is that it can become too legalistic and become more like a bill that needs to be paid. Our tithe to the church could be like paying a condo association fee. Our church participation and offerings will then be like paying membership dues. If our giving becomes drudgery, we are giving for the wrong reason, and we will not experience the joy of giving. The New Testament speaks to our spirituality and how we are to faithfully respond and use our money.

There is a story about a financially successful man who had trouble with the tithing concept. He went to his pastor and said, "If I would tithe my $500,000 salary, I would have to give $50,000." The pastor listened to his problem and agreed that $50,000 was a lot of money to give, so he offered to pray for the man: "Dear Lord, please help my friend earn less money so he finds it easier to tithe."

Balancing Tithing and Grace Giving

Tithing started under God's law, one purpose of which is to show us how sinful we are: "Through the law we become conscious of sin" (Romans 3:20). However, while the law identifies and shows us our errors of action and inaction, God's grace offers forgiveness for our offenses and opens our hearts so that the Holy Spirit may work in us.

God motivates us for stewardship by giving the Gospel—His grace. Stewardship can have no other foundation than the Gospel of forgiveness and God's promises. Grace sets a higher standard for us to achieve as we live and give.

Grace giving often prompts a greater response than the tithe. After Zacchaeus' meeting with a forgiving Savior, he was a new creation and his loving heart caused him to give much more than 10 percent. "But Zacchaeus stood up and said to the Lord, 'Look, Lord! Here and now I give half of my possessions to the poor' " (Luke 19:8).

As recipients of God's blessings we have the responsibility to protect, multiply, and manage God's money for His benefit. Money is only a tool that God places in our hands over which we have temporary custody.

Almost daily we do something with money. We buy, sell, save, give, invest, spend, or plan the use of our money. The activities will vary depending on the amount of money we have and our attitude toward it.

Our uses of and attitudes toward money may cause the biggest challenges and obstacles we face in our spiritual growth. The love of money and possessions is such a great temptation that we are often lost in its grip. The fascination of money is so compelling that God singled out the curse money can be when He said in Matthew 6:24, "You cannot serve both God and Money." If money becomes our focus, we will not find true peace and contentment.

True wisdom with money begins by accepting God's ownership, and that wisdom provides the framework for other financial disciplines. Faithful stewardship promotes good planning, spending, budgeting, investing, and managing of God's money.

Questions for Personal Reflection

This chapter on stewardship is intentionally placed first so a proper foundation can be built for the chapters that follow. Use the following questions to help you focus on your understanding of stewardship.

1. To me, being a good steward means _____.

2. My stewardship involves _____.

3. As a steward I am struggling with _____.

4. What do we mean when we say, "How much of God's money shall I keep?"

5. What does it mean to be "giving under grace" rather than "giving under the law"?

6. Explain why stewardship can be defined as "living all of life for God's purposes."

7. How does your giving help your spiritual growth?

8. In Malachi 3:8–10, what does God say the Israelites are doing when they don't tithe?

9. Read Luke 19:1–10. What was necessary for Zacchaeus before he was willing to give?

10. What principles about the proper use of money can be drawn from the story of Jesus' dealings with Zacchaeus?

11. Read Luke 21:1–4. Was Jesus paying attention to what was given?

12. Why was Jesus commending the widow for giving two small coins when the wealthy were giving big amounts?

13. Read 1 Kings 17:8–24. What was the result of her sacrificial giving?

14. What does sacrificial giving mean to you?

Chapter 2

Planning and Preparing for Our Financial Futures

Planning gives us direction and motivation to accomplish our goals. We plan so we can be initiators, not responders.

May He give you the desire of your heart and make all your plans succeed.
Psalm 20:4

We live in rather strange times. We're always on the run—but often not sure where we're going. We take care of the urgent, focusing only on the pressures of the day. Often, we don't accomplish our goals because we didn't take time to set them. Without a plan, we become reactors or responders rather than action initiators.

> A man driving through the Black Hills near Mount Rushmore ran into a snowstorm and lost all sense of direction. Then he peered out his side window and saw a snowplow. Relieved, he kept as close to the vehicle as he could while it removed snow from the pavement. At times the heavy snowfall made it difficult to follow the machine.
>
> After a while the plow stopped and the operator got out and walked over to the car. "Mister, where are you headed?" the driver asked.
>
> "I'm on my way to Montana," the man responded.
>
> "Well, you'll never get there following me. I'm plowing out this parking lot!"[9]

Are you going nowhere financially? Plan wisely and develop a financial plan which has a purpose and direction that honors God and provides for your needs.

Following God's Plan

We can't separate our finances from our daily walk with Christ because financial decisions are spiritual decisions. When our finances are under control, our Christian ministry has a better chance to grow.

Financial chaos and uncertainty cause anxiety and frustration that can lead to despair. With our lives out of balance because of poor financial planning and management, the potential exists for us to lose our effective witness for Christ. In John 17:4 Jesus said, "I have brought You glory on earth by completing the work You gave me to do." God calls each of us to different vocations and whatever our position, He has a plan for us. We are to work that plan: "Whatever you do, work at it with all your heart, as working for the Lord, not for men" (Colossians 3:23).

In the gospel of Luke, God calls a rich man a fool when he does not include God and concern for others in his plans:

Someone in the crowd said to Him, "Teacher, tell my brother to divide the inheritance with me."

Jesus replied, "Man, who appointed Me a judge or arbiter between you?" Then He said to them, "Watch out! Be on your guard against all kinds of greed; a man's life does not consist in the abundance of his possessions."

And He told them this parable: "The ground of a certain rich man produced a good crop. He thought to himself, 'What shall I do? I have no place to store my crops.'

Then he said, 'This is what I'll do. I will tear down my barns and build bigger ones, and there I will store all my grain and my goods. And I'll say to myself, "You have plenty of good things laid up for many years. Take life easy; eat, drink and be merry." '

"But God said to him, 'You fool! This very night your life will be demanded from you. Then who will get what you have prepared for yourself?'

"This is how it will be with anyone who stores up things for himself but is not rich toward God. ... For where your treasure is, there your heart will be also."
Luke 12:13–21, 34

Accepting the lesson of the parable will give us a proper foundation because God in His infinite wisdom will direct our planning. The rich man was not a good steward. By worldly standards he was successful, but he did not acknowledge that (1) God owns all things, (2) he only managed God's possessions, (3) he was to serve God and his fellow man, and (4) he should thank God for his blessings. Prosperity and wealth without God are worth nothing because the only meaningful wealth is found in Christ.

Jesus did not condemn the man because of his wealth. The problem was not his money but his focus and attitude toward it. His only interest was for more and bigger barns. He wasn't content with what he had. The amount of riches we have does not keep us from loving God, but an abundance of wealth sometimes causes a person to put security in money.

Failing to Plan

Failing to plan can be costly. Without careful planning, we may pay higher federal and state income taxes than we need to or not have enough money for education or retirement. Failing to plan may leave us unprotected from automobile, home, or work-related accidents. Most important, a lack of planning presents the possibility of our inability to reach our God-given goals and potential. To achieve God's goals, we need plans that will provide for protection, growth, and a future. God already has those plans: " 'For I know the plans I have for you,' declares the LORD, 'plans to prosper you and not to harm you, plans to give you hope and a future' " (Jeremiah 29:11).

As the old saying goes, "People don't plan to fail, they fail to plan." Perhaps we don't plan because we don't know how. We may not want to plan because it could involve considering unpleasant events such as debt, unemployment, disability, and death. Examining how we've spent God's money can bring feelings of guilt when we think of our past mistakes. We may feel we do not have enough assets or income even to bother with planning. However, the amount of money doesn't matter. We can misuse our God-given financial gifts whatever their size.

Perhaps we don't even know how or where to begin and need help. We may think a financial planning service may be too expensive, but that's not always true. Besides, many people don't need professional guidance. We may find within our own churches knowledgeable Christians who can provide the financial counsel we need. "Listen to advice and accept instruction, and in the end you will be wise. Many are the plans in a man's heart, but it is the LORD'S purpose that prevails" (Proverbs 19:20–21).

Finally, we may not want to plan because a plan places limits on us and makes us accountable. In the parable of the talents, Jesus reminds us that the master held his three slaves accountable for what they did with the talents he gave them. As caretakers of God's property, we are accountable to Him for all we have.

The story of Joseph (beginning in Genesis 37) offers some insight about the importance of caretaking and planning. Because Joseph planned ahead, Egypt did not have to suffer. Joseph interpreted Pharaoh's dream that Egypt was to have seven years of abundant crops followed by seven years of famine. Joseph, with Pharaoh's authority, developed a plan to store food during the good years so the nation could survive the drought and famine. Joseph's plans saved Egypt. God gave Joseph the wisdom to plan and set goals, and He gives us that same ability.

Setting Goals

A goal is simply a measurable objective toward which you believe God wants you to move. A goal is more than "Wouldn't it be nice if ..." or "I'd really like to have ..." A goal can be measured so you know if it has been accomplished. Goals need to be realistic, practical, and attainable with deadlines. (Happiness, wealth, and success are not goals in themselves but are by-products of goal setting.) By setting goals, you are forced to think through exactly what your financial objectives are. With goals to keep you focused, you are less likely to be sidetracked.

With realistic financial goals you can measure progress. The following are examples of goals that show cost and time frame:

- Provide two children with four years of college education at a cost today of $12,000 each beginning in the years 2000 and 2004.

- Save $30,000 by age 35; $40,000 by age 40; and $60,000 by age 45.

- Buy a new piano in two years at a cost of $3,000.

- Pay off credit card debt of $2,000 by the end of the year.

Financial goals do not remain static but change as circumstances change. A young adult's goals are different from a middle-aged or retired person's goals. Each and every goal needs prayerful consideration. God promises in Proverbs 16:3, "Commit to the LORD whatever you do, and your plans will succeed." God will always be with us. "In his heart a man plans his course, but the LORD determines his steps" (Proverbs 16:9).

Planning and setting goals require some uninterrupted private time, attention, and serious commitment. Both the goals and the plans to reach those goals need to be written down—written goals make us more accountable and provide personal motivation.

The importance of written goals and deadlines was once demonstrated by a Harvard graduating class. A study showed that only five percent of the graduates had written goals, 80 percent had no specific goals, and 15 percent had goals but had not committed them to paper. The five percent who had written down their goals were measured by net assets after 30 years. They had not only surpassed the goals they had written for themselves, but, as a group, had more net worth than the other 95 percent combined.[10]

When you have identified and written down your goals, develop plans to implement them. In financial planning, a goal of many years begins with the first month. Write down both a beginning date and a completion date for your plans and goals.

What goals are important? Pray for guidance as you prioritize your goals. Remember, financial goals need to be specific. "Save money" isn't a goal. "Save $500 in the next 6 months" is a goal. Are you prepared to reexamine your goals periodically and modify them if necessary? Are you willing to take some small risks? Don't let fear, time constraints, lack of knowledge, or the discomfort of staying accountable to a plan paralyze your activities.

Goal-setting Principles

Study the following Scripture references to deepen your understanding of biblical goal-setting principles. Take notes as you study.

Seek first the kingdom of God.

Matthew 6:33 _____

Proverbs 27:24 _____

Seek/accept counsel from Christians.

Psalm 1:1–2 _____

Isaiah 30:1 _____

Proverbs 14:7 _____

Proverbs 19:21 _____

Control self-serving interests.

Proverbs 11:28 _____

Luke 8:14 _____

Proverbs 15:27 _____

Proverbs 25:27 _____

Set objectives to focus your thoughts on accomplishing your goals.

Proverbs 13:22 _____

Proverbs 14:15 _____

Philippians 3:14 _____

Serve God through your wealth.

Proverbs 14:24 _____

2 Corinthians 9:8 _____

1 Timothy 6:18 _____

Share the goals with your entire family.

Proverbs 23:22 _____

Proverbs 13:1 _____

Shape your goals as Solomon did.

1 Kings 3:5–14 _____

Write down your goals and plans.

Proverbs 16:9 _____

Set a time line for meeting your goals.

Luke 14:28–33 _____

Strive for patience and caution.

Proverbs 21:29 _____

Proverbs 24:3–4 _____

Stay flexible.

Matthew 4:19–20 _____

Now take a few minutes to think about your goals and write them down. Answer the following questions once you have written down your goals.

Short-term Goals
(i.e. start savings plan, acquire additional insurance, pay off credit cards)

Long-term Goals
(i.e. retire at age 62, purchase retirement property)

Goal-setting questions

1. What obstacles or problems might you encounter? (Have you collected all relevant data? Are you willing to overcome obstacles to achieve your goals?)

2. What additional training or skills do you need? How much additional time and money will the training take?

3. What additional resources will you need? (Educational reading and training material may be essential.)

4. How much money will it take to reach your goals? Project your future income and expenditure needs.

5. Are there other ways to accomplish your goals? If so, list them.

6. Are your action plans in writing? If not, write them down. Do you have backup plans? Write them down.

7. What are your time frames to reach your goals?

8. What are the personal benefits of accomplishing your goals?

9. Are you keeping your goals visible so you stay on the right track?[11]

Start Now

Planning for the future begins today. Procrastination is one of the greatest hindrances to financial planning, and it's a malady from which most people suffer to some degree. But Galatians 6 reminds us that we reap what we sow. If you sow nothing (that is, don't plan), you reap nothing. If you sow too late, you reap a smaller harvest or run the risk of crop failure. Best intentions get you nowhere. You may be a procrastinator if, when faced with financial planning, you've said:

- ‣ I don't have time right now.

- ‣ I don't know how to put a plan together.

- ‣ I'll do it at the beginning of the new year.

- ‣ I have too much other stuff to worry about.

- ‣ I don't have enough money to do financial planning.

- ‣ I'm too young to worry about that. I'll do it later.

You're never too young to develop a financial plan. And in the end, procrastination can cost you thousands of dollars.

Where Are You Now?

A key in formulating financial plans and goals is determining your current financial condition. The best way to measure your current resources is to calculate your net worth. A net worth calculation clearly shows you your assets and liabilities. The net worth of an individual or family is the dollar value remaining when assets are totaled and, from that figure, liabilities are subtracted. If the assets are less than the liabilities, there may be pending financial crisis. Take some time to fill out the following net worth worksheet.

Net Worth Statement

Date:_____

Fill in the blanks with the most current information you have. The more accurate you can be, the more realistic the net worth totals will be.

What I Own

Liquid Assets:

Checking Account _____

Bank Savings _____

Money Market Funds

_____

Cash Value of Life
Insurance _____

Other _____

Investment Assets:

Mutual Funds _____

Real Estate Investments _____

Antiques _____

Collectibles _____

IRAs _____

401(k) or 403(b) _____

Other _____

Personal Assets:

Residence _____

Household Furnishings _____

Vehicles _____

Boats _____

Other _____

Total Assets: _____

What I Owe

Credit Card Debt _____

Installment Loans _____

Personal Loans _____

Home Mortgage _____

Other _____

Total Liabilities: _____

Total Assets:	_____
Total Liabilities:	− _____
Net Worth:	= _____

The size of your net worth (everything you own) is an important factor in evaluating your financial health. Look back at your list of assets. Did you notice what *types* of assets you have? Assets that can be converted to cash in one year or less are called short-term assets. (Short-term assets include CDs, stocks, bonds, mutual funds, money-market accounts, and the like.) It is important to have enough cash (at least three months of income) in short-term assets to be prepared for emergencies. And that reserve should be readily accessible.

In your financial review process, examine both current and potential future income levels. Factor in taxes and debt as well. Think carefully about your lifestyle. Calculate the expenses you incur in supporting your lifestyle. Do you eat out several times a week? Do you subscribe to multiple pay-stations on cable? Do you belong to book, record, or other mail-order clubs? Are you a list-maker or an impulse buyer when you go shopping? Each of these items figures into the amount of money you need to support your lifestyle. After you review such expenses, you'll have a better understanding of what you need to do to accomplish your short- and long-term goals. Are they necessary or merely habitual? How useful are they? You may think, "$20 per month is peanuts. Cutting that won't help me save for the *future*." But you'd be surprised what $20 per month (that's $240 per year) can do in the right investment plan.

Your planning process should also include "what if" projections such as "What if I'm disabled?" "What if I want to retire in 10 years?" "What if I get a 15 percent return on my investments?" Such planning may seem overly pessimistic to some, but before you start a project, it's wise to sit down and consider what you are going to need to do your work:

> Suppose one of you wants to build a tower. Will he not first sit down and estimate the cost to see if he has enough money to complete it? For if he lays the foundation and is not able to finish it, everyone who sees it will ridicule him, saying, "This fellow began to build and was not able to finish."
>
> Or suppose a king is about to go to war against another king. Will he not first sit down and consider whether he is able with ten thousand men to oppose the one coming against him with twenty thousand? If he is not able, he will send a delegation while the other is still a long way off and will ask for terms of peace. Luke 14:28–33

Budgeting as Planning

Budgeting helps you make intelligent and responsible decisions about the best possible use of your money. A budget is simply a written plan that identifies your spending priorities. A budget can help you see where your money is going and it can help you decide where and how much you can spend. Some folks need to live on a very tight paycheck-to-paycheck budget, where every penny counts. Others have the luxury of a looser budget. Either way, we remain stewards of God's resources and can benefit from a plan for controlling our spending. The word *budget* has become almost as unpleasant as *diet* to many of us—it's a have-to, not a want-to. But budgeting can empower you to use your money more wisely. Budgeting isn't for wimps. It requires action, discipline, and commitment to make it work. And it will likely require sacrifices, such as saying no to or delaying fun purchases. But a budget doesn't have to be painful. The financial goal of a budget is to enjoy a reasonably comfortable lifestyle and to live within your means. Budgets tend to work best when they are a family affair. Open communication is key to keeping your budget. If you plan carefully with your spouse and speak openly with each other about your financial concerns, fears, and ideals, you stand a much better chance of developing a family commitment to your financial goals.

The Budget Process

Step 1: Determine how much money you receive in earnings through work and other sources (such as child support, social security, inheritance, etc.). Add up three months of all sources of income and divide by three for your average monthly income.

Step 2: Calculate your present level of spending, both variable and fixed expenses. Variable expenses are those that vary each month, such as the electric bill, the phone bill, the grocery bill. Fixed expenses are those that do not change, such as the mortgage payment and car payment. Do you tithe? That figures in here as well. When you have determined your sources of income and expenses, you will be able to construct a cash flow analysis that will show you if you are living within your means and what your priorities are.

Step 3: Determine your priorities and the amount of money you will spend. Setting priorities and sticking to the budget helps prevent impulse spending. The cash flow analysis in step 2 will show you where your spending leaks are. Are there large chunks of money unaccounted for? Not many people keep track of every penny of loose change they spend, but did you realize that drinking one can of soda each day at 75¢ per can adds up to $273.75 per year? That's a lot of incidental spending when you look at the big picture.

Write down a monthly estimate for each category of spending, such as car payments, clothing, food, entertainment, etc. Each month, add up what you actually spent in each category and compare that to your budgeted amount (estimate). If your expenses are larger than your budget estimates, you'll need to make some adjustments. The adjustment could be to raise the monthly budgeted amount, but it will most likely need to be cutting spending. It's important that your list include all expenditures. You'll be surprised what you spend in some areas.

To set up your categories for your budget, you may want to purchase budget forms (which can be found in most office supply stores) or you may want to invest in computer software. Many of the software packages on the market make setting up the budget and running reports fairly simple, even if you're neither a financial nor a computer whiz.

Step 4: Establish a budget that is both rigid and flexible. Some expenses are fixed; others, such as entertainment, can be changed. Avoid spending all your "extra" money on unnecessary items. Be sure to include in your budget plans for upcoming major purchases and expenses. Is the dishwasher getting old? Will it need to be replaced in the next year or so? Plan for that in your budget. When will your car need a new set of tires? Is that in the budget or is it going to hit you hard in the entertainment pocket? You'll grow to hate budgeting if necessary expenses, such as a complete tune-up or new set of tires, aren't part of the budget, and you have to sacrifice fun things to pay for them. Plan ahead and those expenses won't hurt as much. Planning ahead for such incidental expenses can also keep you from dipping into savings too frequently or using credit unwisely.

Remember that a budget is a fluid document. If you set your budget before you had children, revise it. Children will completely change your financial priorities and budget needs. When the children leave home, the budget needs another overhaul. Any major life change—residence relocation, job change, salary increase, elderly parents coming to live with you, a serious illness or accident—will cause changes in your spending and saving patterns. Be ready for them and be flexible enough to adjust your budget to accommodate them.

Protect Yourself

If you don't have a plan, you are susceptible to making mistakes and doing foolish things. There are several ways a good plan can offer protection:

1. *Planning will reduce or prevent impulse buying.* The window-shopping or mall-walking pastimes that we enjoy make us vulnerable to impulse buying—buying things we don't need or spending too much on something because it's convenient. By sticking to a plan, we are less likely to buy things that aren't in the budget. Impulse buying can easily add $10 or $20 to your grocery bill. Making a list and using coupons, conversely, can save you that much.

2. *Planning can force you to set priorities.* Planning and prayer can help you set a proper course for your spending. When we listen for the Lord's guidance before we make plans, we are protected from misplaced priorities.

3. *Planning can protect you from debt.* With a plan in place, you can reduce or eliminate hasty and improper buying decisions. All purchases should be part of the plan.

4. *Planning will help you achieve your goals.* Without plans and goals, you tend to spend money on your biggest impulse or where you receive the most pressure. Without a plan, it's difficult to say no to desires. Focus on being proactive instead of reactive with your God-given money.

5. *Planning will help you properly use your God-given possessions.* All our possessions are gifts from God and should be properly protected from waste. We save money when we stretch the usefulness of what we already own.[12]

Preparing for the Future

The motto of the Boy Scouts, "Be Prepared," is a good one for both our financial and spiritual lives. The parable of the 10 virgins illustrates the importance of preparation:

> At that time the kingdom of heaven will be like ten virgins who took their lamps and went out to meet the bridegroom. Five of them were foolish and five were wise. The foolish ones took their lamps but did not take any oil with them. The wise, however, took oil in jars along with their lamps. The bridegroom was a long time in coming, and they all became drowsy and fell asleep.

At midnight the cry rang out: "Here's the bridegroom! Come out to meet him!"

Then all the virgins woke and trimmed their lamps. The foolish ones said to the wise, "Give us some of your oil; our lamps are going out."

"No," they replied, "there may not be enough for both us and you. Instead go to those who sell oil and buy some for yourselves." But while they were on their way to buy the oil, the bridegroom arrived. The virgins who were ready went in with him to the wedding banquet. And the door was shut.

Later the others also came, "Sir! Sir!" they said, "Open the door for us!"

But he replied, "I tell you the truth, I do not know you." Therefore keep watch, because you do not know the day or the hour. Matthew 25:1–13

Unfortunately, because five of the bridesmaids had not planned ahead, they missed the wedding celebration. They failed to plan and they suffered the consequences. God has truly blessed us with a tremendous amount of resources. We can enjoy satisfaction and achievement with them or squander them. If the foolish bridesmaids in the parable had known when the groom was coming, they would have brought more oil. It's our responsibility to plan for the unknown and unexpected. Because our world is unpredictable, preparation is key.

But all the planning and preparing in the world can't offer complete security. In truth, there is only one source of security, Jesus Christ, the Bridegroom. When the stock market fluctuates, when our plans don't work out, when we don't meet the budget, Christ remains our foundation, the solid rock on which we stand.

Questions for Personal Reflection

Use the following questions to help you focus on your understanding of planning and preparation.

Read the parable of the rich fool, Luke 12:13–21, 34.

1. Was it wrong for the wealthy farmer to be planning ahead?

2. Should the man be ashamed of his success?

3. Was it OK for the farmer to be building new barns?

4. What was the attitude of the rich man toward his possessions?

5. What was the farmer planning to do during his retirement?

6. Why was the farmer foolish?

7. How does the parable apply to your life?

8. How is a Christian wealthy?

Read the parable of the 10 virgins, Matthew 25:1–13.

9. How were five of the bridesmaids affected by not planning ahead?

10. How is the Boy Scouts' motto, "Be Prepared," applicable to this parable?

11. How does this parable apply to your life?

A goal is simply a measurable objective toward which you believe God wants you to move. Goals need deadlines so progress can be measured. For example, a measurable goal might be to save $12,000 for college tuition in four years' time. To accomplish your goals, you need resolve, determination, and commitment.

12. What improper goal does 1 Timothy 6:9–10 discuss?

13. According to Matthew 28:18–20, what is God's priority goal for you?

14. Why does God want you to be a good planner and wise money manager?

Chapter 3

Money Wise

To be wise managers of money we need discipline, goals, and knowledge. We are called to be faithful and responsible with the money God has entrusted to us.

Command those who are rich in this present world not to be arrogant
nor to put their hope in wealth, which is so uncertain, but to put their hope in God,
who richly provides us with everything for our enjoyment. 1 Timothy 6:17

We can give, save, or spend our money. How much we give, save, or spend indicates a lot about our values and interests. Are you willing to give 10 percent to the church? Is saving important to you? Do you need to have nice things? Our Christian values help us determine the wise use of our money.

As a Christian, a beginning goal is to allocate your money in a 10–10–80 ratio: give 10 percent, save 10 percent, and live on the remaining 80 percent. The first portion goes to the Lord as a thank offering for all He has given to us: "Bring the best of the firstfruits of your soil to the house of the LORD your God" (Exodus 23:19). God defines the tithe, or 10th, in Leviticus 27:30, "A tithe of everything from the land, whether grain from the soil or fruit from the trees, belongs to the LORD; it is holy to the LORD." Giving becomes possible when our hearts are filled with gratitude for God's love, sacrifice, and generosity. Giving is a natural response from a loving heart. When we experience the joy and blessings of giving, we may even want to give beyond the 10 percent.

Put the second 10 percent in savings. In order to develop some financial liquidity and to accomplish your short- and long-term goals, develop a savings plan—a methodical discipline of putting money aside for the future. With the savings you accumulate, consider an investment strategy that provides adequate growth without undue risk. To make future goals possible, current sacrifices may need to be made. Save to pay for educational opportunities, retirement business ventures, and trips you dream about. Save for things you can't anticipate such as calamities or once-in-a-lifetime opportunities. To achieve the savings you want, consider the following savings approach.

1. *Increased Saving*. Having well-defined goals (along with the money needed to accomplish them) can help motivate you to increase your saving. If you want to have a comfortable lifestyle, to be free of debt, educate your children, and live comfortably in retirement, you need a disciplined savings program. Any amount of saving is better than none. If you invest $20 per week for 20 years and receive 12 percent per year (from mutual fund investments), the investment will grow to nearly $86,000. By saving $3,500 per year beginning at age 20, at seven percent, you could have in excess of $1,000,000 at age 65.

A simple way to calculate how long it takes for savings to double is the rule of 72. The time in years is determined by dividing the interest rate that savings are receiving, or will in the future receive, into 72. For example, if you receive eight percent on your investments, it will take nine years for your money to double ($72 \div 8 = 9$). The compounding of interest has a profound effect on how much savings you will have at retirement. For example, if you start with a $5,000 savings and an interest rate of eight percent, you achieve the following:

$5,000 at age 25

10,000 at age 34

20,000 at age 43

40,000 at age 52

80,000 at age 61

160,000 at age 70

You work for your money, and your money can work for you. A solid savings plan will ensure that your money will work just as hard for you as you have worked to acquire it.

2. *Systematic Saving*. More savings can be accumulated through a disciplined, habitual saving approach than if you save only unplanned excesses. You might be able to afford to put $100 into a savings plan at the first of every month; however, if you wait to save what is left over at the end of the month, there may not be anything to save. For savings to become a reality, treat your saving as a regular expense and give it high priority. To make saving more systematic, you may choose to have a mutual fund company take automatic withdrawals from your checking account. Once you begin the program, it perpetuates itself until you make an effort to stop it. In Proverbs, Solomon related how we can learn from the wisdom of ants who store their provisions from today's bounty for future use: "Go to the ant, you sluggard; consider its ways and be wise! It has no commander, no overseer or ruler, yet it stores its provisions in summer and gathers its food at harvest" (Proverbs 6:6–8). It's simple for us to do the same.

48

3. *Tax-Advantaged Saving.* Two advantages are available for saving on taxes with earnings from work. The first is the ability to save pretax money by having earnings invested and not paying income tax initially on that income. It is to your advantage to have 100 percent of the money from earnings through work invested, not just the amount remaining after taxes. A second tax advantage is having the investment income in the account grow tax deferred. You do not eliminate the taxes, but you delay paying the taxes until a future date.

A qualified retirement account that provides both advantages described above is a 401(k) plan (or 403(b) if you work for a nonprofit organization). Monthly amounts are deducted from your gross earnings and invested. The amount deducted from your gross income and the earnings on the investment avoid current taxation. An individual retirement account (IRA) provides similar tax advantages, but there are restrictions on the amount that can be taken as a current tax deduction. With an IRA, tax can be deferred until age 70½, at which time a portion of the principal needs to be withdrawn each year. Because of the tax savings, retirement funds should be invested first in IRAs and 401(k) plans. Money will grow much faster when taxes can be paid at a later date. Note

that there is a 10 percent penalty for withdrawing money from a qualified retirement plan (either an IRA or 401(k)) before age 59½; avoid putting all your savings in those plans.

4. *Smart Saving*. You can choose to settle for returns as small as money market returns or reach for greater, but riskier, returns through stocks and bonds. You can also invest your money in real estate or collectibles, but for most investors the largest portion of their nonbank investing will be done in stocks and bonds. Smart saving begins with using the allowed tax-advantage investment vehicles, then investing in select mutual funds or stocks for appreciation. To invest wisely, you will have to spend some time and effort to educate yourself to become a knowledgeable investor.

By not saving, you will lose opportunities to increase your wealth because your money is not working for you in a compounding investment. Money that you save can be working for you 24 hours a day, seven days a week. Almost everyone can find some painless ways of freeing up some money to save. Here are some ways to reduce spending and make money available for saving. Assuming an eight percent return for 25 years, these are approximate amounts of savings you can expect:

Spend $2,500 less on a car	(total savings)	$17,122
Stop smoking	($4.50 per day savings)	$130,176
Brown-bag lunch 2 days/week	($10 per week savings)	$41,208
Don't buy lottery tickets	($25 per month savings)	$23,776
Stop after-work socializing	($50 per month savings)	$47,551
Don't adopt a pet dog	($25 per month savings)	$23,776
		$283,609

If you don't smoke, drink, go on elaborate vacations, or develop poor spending habits, you greatly improve your potential for saving money. Closely examine your habits, especially those you think of as costing you very little. Could you get along without them? If you went to happy hour with your friends after work once a month instead of every Friday, how much could you save? Don't "punish" yourself or do away with all of your fun incidental spending. But be aware of what you are sacrificing by keeping those habits.

Setting goals gives you a purpose for saving. Having goals can also make saving fun. If you assign amounts and dates to your goal setting, your chances of success improve.

Goal	Total Cost	Target Date	# of Months	Monthly Savings Needed
New Car				
Piano				
Vacation				
College				
House				

Choosing a Lifestyle

If you follow the 10–10–80 principle, what type of lifestyle should the 80 percent that you live on provide? Are you pleasing God by living in substandard housing, driving broken-down used cars, wearing cheap clothes, and not satisfying any of your desires? Is God happy if you have an abundance of nice things? God does not list the specifics on the type of home, car, or clothes we are to have, but He does give us principles:

Therefore I tell you, do not worry about your life, what you will eat or drink; or about your body, what you will wear. Is not life more important than food, and the body more important than clothes? Look at the birds of the air; they do not sow or reap or store away in barns, and yet your heavenly Father feeds them. Are you not much more valuable than they? Who of you by worrying can add a single hour to his life?

And why do you worry about clothes? See how the lilies of the field grow. They do not labor or spin. Yet I tell you that not even Solomon in all his splendor was dressed like one of these. If that is how God clothes the grass of the field, which is here today and tomorrow is thrown into the fire, will He not much more clothe you, O you of little faith? So do not worry, saying, "What shall we eat?" or "What shall we drink?" or "What shall we wear?" For the pagans run after all these things, and your heavenly Father knows that you need them. But seek first His kingdom and His righteousness, and all these things will be given to you as well. Therefore do not worry about tomorrow, for tomorrow will worry about itself. Each day has enough trouble of its own. Matthew 6:25–34

Does your lifestyle reflect your relationship with Christ? There is a tremendous amount of diversity among Christians and what they own. If we have comfortable homes, new cars, fashionable clothes, etc., we can serve and love the Lord as much as someone in poverty. God does not condemn being rich, but He speaks against the self-centered attitude wealth can cause. If an individual acquires her wealth in a proper way and devotes herself and her resources to Christ, God is not going to be disappointed that she lives comfortably.

However, if a person's lifestyle is wasteful and opulent, that violates God's stewardship principles. There is nothing wrong with being rich, but God warns in 1 Timothy 6:9, "People who want to get rich fall into temptation and a trap and into many foolish and harmful desires that plunge men into ruin and destruction." Our culture promotes monetary wealth. Be careful not to become victim of the foolish desires money can create. Satan works on us daily and attempts to convince us we need more and more.

You've probably heard about the experiment that involved placing a frog in a kettle of room temperature water. The comfortable frog sat there, oblivious to the steadily rising temperature of the water as it was being heated. It didn't take long before the frog, sitting contentedly in now near-boiling water, expired without ever realizing what was happening. We too can have a similar experience with a materialistic lifestyle that grows gradually as needs are met, desires are attained, and a covetous attitude begins to take over. Just like the contented frog, without our noticing what is happening, our interests become so fixated on "things" of the world that we are in danger of spiritual and financial expiration. This attitude and lifestyle does not occur quickly, for just as the frog dropped into already boiling water springs immediately out of the kettle, so we, when aware, avoid the dangers of greed.

Overcoming Money Problems

God has given us possessions over which we are managers but we may have developed bad habits, received poor advice, encountered some misfortunes, or made foolish mistakes with our money. Without control of our financial situations, we will struggle and possible suffer because of money-related problems. These problems can damage or even destroy a marriage—financial troubles are cited as the cause of most divorces. The five main money traps found in marriages are:

- ▸ too much impulse buying (splurging)
- ▸ spending too much on the house
- ▸ spending too much on the car
- ▸ a growing, expensive hobby
- ▸ a desire to overindulge children or grandchildren

And these traps are symptoms of other typical money problems:

Get-rich-quick attitude. Every year, thousands risk and lose money they can't afford to lose while seeking that "big deal." This attitude is both sneaky and pervasive, popping up everywhere from gambling boats to infomercials to your own mailbox. Gambling boats and casinos are perhaps the most obvious—you know what you're getting into and just hope it'll be your lucky day. The others are more subtle. They promise that you can make a lot of money quickly if you just buy into their plan or partner in their "business." The promise of easy money is very tempting, but chances are you won't be the one making the easy money—the folks tempting you will be.

Procrastination. Time is precious gift from God. Wasting it is wasting an opportunity to be a good steward. Procrastination can be costly as well. For example, a 28-year-old who invests $2,000 for seven years at 10 percent has an investment value at age 65 of $400,000. If that person waits until he is 35 to start investing the $2,000 per year until retirement, he will only acquire the same amount as the 28-year-old who only invested for seven years. The earlier you invest your money, the greater your benefit from compounding interest.

Covetousness. A materialistic attitude is a real roadblock to good stewardship and generous giving. Don't be fooled into thinking that only really greedy people can covet. Our society encourages us to covet every day. But Scripture would have us think otherwise: "For the love of money is a root of all kinds of evil. Some people, eager for money, have wandered from the faith and pierced themselves with many griefs" (1 Timothy 6:10).

Disorganization. Unless you took accounting classes, you probably haven't had formal training in money management. Some people organize their finances the way they saw their parents do it, others had no role model at all. If your financial records are disorganized, you're less likely to spend time focusing on finances. But rest assured that poor organization can be corrected with discipline, education and planning.

Lack of financial knowledge. Handling money is a big part of your life. If you don't know that much about your finances—from what you should look for in a checking account to solid investment techniques—you probably need to sharpen your skills. Read books, attend workshops, classes, or seminars, and seek out others who are money wise.

Lack of commitment. Once you become knowledgeable and organized, keep it up. After you've set plans and goals, revisit them periodically. If you're married, you and your spouse can have a system of checks and balances where you keep each other committed to the task.

Pride. Many of us have a problem with pride and don't even realize it. We get caught up in the achievement spiral and become boastful and indulgent. Pray daily that pride won't creep into your life and take you over.

These are the most typical money problems we face each day. Be honest with yourself about which of them affect you. Then pray and write down a plan to overcome the obstacle.

Tax Planning

To be money wise, it is essential that you understand our tax system—the biggest expense in your lifetime will likely be the taxes you pay. In Matthew 22:21, Jesus said, "Give to Caesar what is Caesar's, and to God what is God's." As Christians we are obligated to pay our taxes, but we need not pay more than our share. Tax avoidance is a legal way to reduce your taxes. It simply requires that you know enough of the tax laws to use them to your advantage. Understanding tax laws is a real challenge because of their complexity and because the laws are always changing. Many taxpayers have given up and have hired professionals to complete their returns—nearly half the 15 million tax returns the IRS received in 1993 were completed by paid preparers. But if you are acquainted with basic tax laws, you can help a professional tax preparer use the laws to keep you from paying unnecessary taxes.

The tax that has the biggest impact on us is the federal personal income tax. The Internal Revenue Service has tax schedules for single taxpayers, for married taxpayers filing jointly, for married taxpayers filing separately, and for heads of households. The taxes you pay will depend on how you file.

The various tax rates you pay are referred to as marginal tax rates. The tax is progressive, which will cause you to pay a higher tax rate as your earnings increase. The highest marginal tax rate is the tax you pay on the last dollars earned after exemptions and deductions. For example, if a person is in a 28 percent marginal tax bracket, she will pay 28 cents in taxes for every dollar of taxable income. If her earnings increase, it may cause the marginal tax bracket to increase to a 31 percent or higher marginal tax rate.

Knowing the marginal tax rate will help a family determine the economics and wisdom for such decisions as having a two-income family. After deducting any expenses and taxes, you can calculate your net income. The added income, however, may push a couple into a higher marginal tax rate.

Until the government taxes 100 percent of what we earn, we need to continue earning as much as we can. You can reduce your taxable income by having more children and increasing your personal exemptions, getting divorced and deducting alimony payments, or withdrawing savings early and deducting the savings penalty. However, none of these is a good tax savings plan. Deductions from earnings that are wise, proper, and make economic sense include charitable contributions, payments to qualified retirement accounts, and home interest deductions. The law allows charitable cash deductions of up to 50 percent of what you earn each year. With a national giving average of approximately three percent per year, the 50 percent deduction limit is of little concern. If you tithe, you should be filing itemized deductions rather than the standard deduction method. If you use a professional tax preparer, make sure he or she is aware of your contributions.

Retirement account opportunities provide one of the best ways to reduce your earnings or taxable income for tax purposes. You can invest in 401(k) or 403(b) plans that allow contributions to be deducted from earnings. For example, if one spouse made $45,000 per year and chose to put $6,000 into a 401(k) plan, the earnings shown on that spouse's W-2 for the year would reflect only $39,000. The $6,000 would be put into a tax-deferred investment account and be subject to tax only when distributed from the plan. The following table shows the advantages over 20 years using a 401(k) automatic payroll deduction plan.

	Ordinary Investment	401(k) Investment
Annual contribution	$6,000	$6,000
28% income tax	$1,680	$0
Actual amount to invest	$4,320	$6,000
Total investment (20 years)	$120,000	$120,000
Value if earning 8% after 20 years in a 28% tax bracket	$197,697	$274,571

For tax advantages, an excellent investment vehicle is an Individual Retirement Account (IRA). Investors in an IRA benefit from being able to defer taxes on any income and growth within an IRA. In addition to deferring taxes, the current tax law allows taxpayers below a given amount of earned income the opportunity to reduce their taxable income by the amount of their IRA contributions, which in effect reduces their current tax liabilities. For example, if a married couple earns $40,000 and invests $2,000 in an IRA, the investment reduces their taxable income to $38,000.

Currently, a wage earner who earns $2,000 or more of income can invest that amount in an IRA. Married couples who only have one wage earner may also invest an additional $2,000 for the nonworking spouse. The deferral advantage exists until the age 70 ½, when each year a portion of the IRA money needs to be withdrawn. Be aware, however, that there is a 10 percent penalty on any money withdrawn from an IRA prior to age 59 ½.

The tax consequences of investments affect the total taxes you pay. The retirement accounts referred to are advantageous because tax consequences on the income and growth of the investments are deferred until the funds are withdrawn. The same tax deferral can be achieved by purchasing deferred annuities. If you purchase tax-free municipal bonds, you can avoid federal tax totally. Investing wisely to avoid taxes can help create tax refunds.

An important tax reduction strategy for many is the ability to deduct the interest on home mortgages. Home ownership is often made economically feasible because you can deduct the interest payments. Also, any borrowing beyond the home mortgage that is absolutely necessary should be done through a tax deductible home-equity loan if available because the IRS does not allow deduction for credit card or installment loan interest.

For some, a tax reduction strategy is to give money ($10,000 per year tax free) to minor children and have the investment income taxed to the children. For children under 14, tax laws require most of the investment income to be taxed to the parents. If the child is 14 or older, tax advantages can be significant because the income is taxed to the children. With children in a lower tax bracket, the family will save on taxes. Following are some tax deductions that you may not know you can take:

- ► Expenses such as financial advice, certain legal and accounting fees, tax preparation costs, and safe-deposit box rental are deductible above a floor amount.

- ► If losses over $100 occur through theft or casualty, which are not covered through insurance, the amount that exceeds 10 percent of the adjusted gross income is deductible.

- ► For dependent family members, such as parents, you can currently take an added exemption deduction if you contribute over half of the person's total support.

- ► If you purchase a home or refinance, you can deduct the "points." Remember, home mortgage interest is deductible.

- ► If you engage an employment agency and incur other costs looking for a new job in your present field, these costs are deductible above a floor amount.

- ► You may deduct subscriptions to professional journals above a floor amount.

- ► Any unreimbursed travel, meal, or entertainment expenses are reimbursed above a floor amount. (The floor amount is currently two percent of adjusted gross income.)

- ► You may deduct mileage for driving to volunteer work.

Protection through Insurance

Becoming money wise includes understanding and using insurance properly. Insurance is the payment of an amount of money, called a premium, in exchange for protection against a larger uncertain cost. Insurance is needed when a potential financial loss could be excessive.

You face risks daily. Without protection, an unforeseen catastrophe could wipe away years of hard work and saving. Death, accidents, illness, property loss, and legal liability are major risks families face. Insurance can give you peace of mind knowing that money will be available to meet the needs of your survivors, pay medical bills, protect your home and belongings, and cover personal and property damage of your cars. There are four ways to protect yourself against risk:

1. *Avoid risk altogether.* You can protect or shield yourself from risk by avoiding it. One way to avoid the risk of a fire in a home would be not to own one.

2. *Reduce the risk.* You can reduce the risk of fire in your home by using smoke alarms. This will reduce but not avoid the risk.

3. *Retain the risk.* For items that are not overly expensive, it may be best not to insure them. If the frequency of the loss is small, and the cost to replace it manageable, retain the risk.

4. *Transfer the risk.* You can transfer the risk to an insurance company by paying premiums.

Does owning an insurance policy show lack of faith? Scripture does not refer specifically to insurance, but Proverbs 27:12 says, "The prudent see danger and take refuge, but the simple keep going and suffer for it." God holds us responsible for His gifts; we are accountable for our families, our livelihoods, and our resources. Good stewardship calls for insurance that has been thoroughly evaluated for its risk protection and cost effectiveness. Any insurance you purchase should be part of an overall plan and bought only after careful review of the reputation, rating, and service of the insurance carrier.

Types of Life Insurance

If your death would cause financial stress for your spouse, children, parents, or anyone else you want to protect, consider purchasing life insurance. Your stage in life and the home you live in will determine your needs. Before you decide to buy or increase your life insurance, you should have a basic understanding of the four main types of life insurance available.

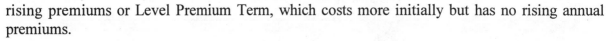

Term life—Provides pure protection only for a specified period of time. This type of policy does not build up cash value. This is the most economical way of purchasing substantial amounts of death protection. You can buy Annually Renewable Term with constant benefits and rising premiums or Level Premium Term, which costs more initially but has no rising annual premiums.

Whole life—This type of policy provides a death protection plus a cash build-up feature. Because of the savings within the policy, the protection is more expensive than term insurance.

Universal life—Universal life is similar to whole life in that it provides a permanent form of life insurance protection. The premium payment is different than whole life because the payments are somewhat flexible. Universal life combines both term and whole life protection.

Variable life—This general kind of cash value insurance differs from whole life and universal life in allowing more leeway in investment choices.

How Much Insurance Is Enough?

Insurance salespeople or underwriters look at your personal situation to give you a recommendation. One rule of thumb is that a person have insurance coverage of five times his or her annual income. A needs analysis that projects future financial needs is a more precise method of determining the recommended amount of insurance, however. Many factors are part of determining how much insurance you need:

- age
- occupation
- work insurance
- health
- gender
- family's financial needs
- number of children
- educational needs
- special needs
- income capability of surviving spouse

A properly trained life insurance agent can factor in all the variables and determine an amount of insurance appropriate for your protection needs. Choosing a good agent is one of the most important steps in purchasing insurance. Following are typical examples of how life insurance proceeds are used:

- paying off a home mortgage or other debts by way of a decreasing term policy
- providing lump-sum payments to children when they reach a specified age
- providing an education or income for children
- making charitable bequests after death
- providing a retirement income
- accumulating savings
- establishing a regular income for survivors
- setting up an estate plan
- making estate and death tax payments

Think carefully about how you intend your life insurance benefits to be used. Then meet with a qualified insurance agent to discuss your insurance needs.

Determining Your Financial Condition

The following questions will help you determine just how money wise you are. Take a moment to answer them.

1. Are you giving a proportionate firstfruits offering to God?

2. Do you identify and share with the needy?

3. Have you made a list of specific financial goals and determined a time frame to achieve those goals?

4. Have you embarked on a savings or an investment program to achieve your goals?

5. Do you have an emergency fund of least three months' salary?

6. Do you have a reasonable amount of money invested in growth?

7. Is all of your money earning interest, including your checking account balance?

8. Do you have a diversified investment portfolio?

9. Are you communicating with your spouse regarding the family finances?

10. Do you have a spending plan?

11. Are you spending less than what you make?

12. Are you saving nearly 10 percent each month?

13. Do you annually compute your net worth?

14. Are you paying your credit card balances each month?

15. Do you have adequate disability, life, health, and property insurance?

16. Are you utilizing your 401(k) or 403(b) and IRA investment opportunities?

17. Do you have an updated will?

18. Does your estate exceed the current unified credit? If so, are you doing some estate tax planning?

Becoming money wise begins by developing a proper attitude. Money can help you acquire many things, but it is not able to give life true meaning. Knowing money can buy health care but not health, a bed but not sleep, a church but not salvation makes a difference in our attitudes toward money. When money, success, and possessions are not the focus of our attention, we've eliminated a major obstacle to living a closer relationship with Christ.

Questions for Personal Reflection

Use the following questions to help you focus on your understanding of being money wise.

1. "Remember this: Whoever sows sparingly will also reap sparingly, and whoever sows generously will also reap generously" (2 Corinthians 9:6). As God's stewards, it is our job to sow wisely. How does the sowing and reaping principle apply to Luke 6:38 and Proverbs 3:9–10?

2. Can you give some examples in other areas of life that if you sow generously you reap generously?

The 10-10-80 Principle

Giving

3. Are we called to give less under God's grace than under the law?

4. What is Jesus saying in Luke 11:42?

5. Does Jesus ever ask for more than 10 percent (Mark 10:21)?

6. Can you think of an example in the New Testament when giving under grace caused greater giving than a tithe?

7. What does God say to the Israelites in Malachi 1:6–10 about giving leftovers or improper gifts?

Saving

8. What is the rule of 72?

9. How can you save systematically?

Lifestyle

10. Are we pleasing God if we live in substandard housing, drive broken-down used cars, wear cheap shoes, and deny our desires? Why?

11. Is God pleased if we have an abundance of nice things (Matthew 6:25–34)?

12. What does Paul warn about in 1 Timothy 6:9 concerning people wanting to be rich so they can live in luxury?

13. What does Jesus say we are not to worry about (Matthew 6:24–34)?

14. What lifestyle pleases God?

Chapter 4

Responsible Money Managers

Challenge yourself daily to be wise in your spending, planning, giving, managing, and investing.

By wisdom a house is built, and through understanding it is established;
through knowledge its rooms are filled with rare and beautiful treasures.
Proverbs 24:3–4

Until we have a good understanding of where our money is going, it's hard to manage it well. If we can't manage it, we can't save it. It we can't save it, we can't invest it. If we can't invest it, we can't make it grow so we can reach our financial goals, create a nice retirement fund, and have funds to share with others.

The biblical concept of stewardship also reveals that we have a responsibility to our families to manage properly the assets God has given us:"If anyone does not provide for his relatives, and especially for his immediate family, he has denied the faith and is worse than an unbeliever" (1 Timothy 5:8). As parents, we have a responsibility to our children to model prudent planning for our futures and theirs.

Developing a Spending Plan

To be prudent and wise with the money you earn, develop a plan to spend your money wisely. A spending plan will help match your income to your expenses, and it is used as a set of guidelines to point you in the direction you want to go. Spending plans are flexible because you have personal control. You determine how much you are going to give, spend, and save.

To determine your spending habits, keep meticulous records for at least two months, noting where and how you've spent your money—you may be surprised. From your list of expenses, separate those that are fixed from those that are variable. Some months you may not have any additional variable expenses at all, but during other months you may incur considerable expense. The secret is to allocate some money every month to cover those expenses.

To figure out how much to set aside for these irregular expenses, average your bills for the past year. For items such as annual or semiannual insurance payments, set aside a monthly reserve so you can pay the premium when it's due without feeling pinched. You do not have a good spending plan unless you allow for expenses that are not due every month.

Here's how to plan for variable expenses:

Category	Annual Estimated Cost	Monthly Cost (Annual Cost ÷ 12)
Life Insurance	$	$
Property Insurance	$	$
Health Insurance	$	$
Auto Insurance	$	$
Clothing	$	$
Doctor	$	$
Dentist	$	$
Automobile(s)	$	$
Vacation	$	$
Gifts	$	$
Home and car expenses	$	$
Home furnishings and appliances	$	$
Other Variable Expenses	$	$

When you set money aside every month, there will be both fewer surprises and fewer financial problems. A key in setting up a spending plan is to expect the unexpected. With a solid spending plan, it won't hurt when you suddenly need to replace the washer or the transmission in your car.

Entertainment and recreation can be costly, variable parts of your spending plan. Tight controls may be necessary. Many people put their monthly entertainment money in an envelope—when the money is gone, the eating out and entertaining stops for the month. Try it—it's a good way to discipline yourself and evaluate how you make entertainment decisions.

So you've figured out how much money is going out and where it's going, how do you figure out how much you actually have to spend? Your monthly cash flow can be determined as follows:

Net Income	(monthly gross income minus taxes)	$
Investment Income	(earnings from investments)	$
Total Spendable Net Income	(add net income and investment income)	$

Charitable Giving	(percentage based on gross income)	$
Savings	(total amount currently in savings)	$
Fixed Expenses	(total of unchanging expenses)	$
Variable Expenses	(total of changing expenses)	$
Total Expenses	(add giving, savings, fixed and variable expenses)	$

Net Monthly Cash Flow	(net income minus giving, saving, and expenses)	$

Due to differences in personal preferences as well as lifestyles and ages, we spend our money in different ways. To set up a spending plan that has a chance of succeeding, be realistic. The plan has to do more than look good on paper; it needs to be in tune with your spending habits.

Ways to Cut Expenses

It is possible to spend less by developing better spending habits and breaking poor ones. Spending less and saving more puts you in a better position to accomplish future goals. Specific ways to spend less:

Cut costs

- Plan shopping in advance and buy only what you plan.
- Increase the deductible on your car insurance.
- Cut your children's hair instead of paying for a salon.
- Shop at garage sales, flea markets, and discount outlets.
- Use fans instead of air conditioning.
- Lower the thermostat during the winter, raise it during the summer. Put it on a timer that adjusts temperature to the time of day.
- Join or form a baby-sitting club.
- Wash the car and change the oil yourself.
- Join a car pool.
- See movies at a discount theater.
- Write letters or use e-mail instead of calling.
- Make handmade gifts.
- Wrap children's gifts in comic paper instead of expensive gift wrap.
- Sew items for the home—curtains, pillows, etc.
- Exchange baby-sitting and pet-sitting favors with a neighbor.
- Return soda cans and bottles.
- Cut vacation costs by going camping.

Food savings

- Buy store-brand or generic-brand products.
- Use coupons.
- Go to the store with the best bargains.
- Don't buy prepared snacks or convenience foods.
- Look for savings on day-old bread.
- Avoid impulse buying. Stick with your shopping list.
- Shop at bulk food stores.
- Mix whole milk with powdered milk.

- Buy less cereal. Supplement with breads, homemade granola, fruit.
- Plant a garden. Can or freeze for the winter.
- Cook in quantity. Freeze meals to avoid fast-food nights.
- Have three meatless evening meals each week.

Saving on clothes

- Shop at discount and thrift stores.
- Shop during sales. Take advantage of off-season sales.
- Avoid fad or trendy clothes when possible.
- Buy and sell at garage sales.
- Take care of clothes.
- Plan your wardrobe before going shopping.
- Buy quality items that look better and last longer.
- Learn to sew.

Proper Spending

Study the following Scripture references to deepen your understanding of biblical principles regarding spending.

Put God first.

Matthew 6:24 _____

Matthew 19:29 _____

Deuteronomy 6:5 _____

Proverbs 3:9 _____

Prepare a budget.

Luke 16:10–11 _____

Luke 14:28–30 _____

Provide for your family.

1 Timothy 5:8 _____

Galatians 6:10 _____

Put a stop to buying with credit.

    Proverbs 22:7 _____

Pay off all debts.

    Psalm 37:21 _____

    Matthew 5:25–26 _____

    Romans 13:8 _____

Plan for inevitable emergency expenditures.

    Proverbs 6:6–8 _____

Place a priority on saving.

    1 Corinthians 16:2 _____

    Luke 19:23 _____

    Proverbs 21:20 _____

Prepare to deny certain wants and desires.

    Proverbs 14:23 _____

    1 John 2:15–16 _____

    Ecclesiastes 2:10–11 _____

Prevent impulse spending.

    Proverbs 21:17 _____

    Proverbs 25:28 _____

    Proverbs 27:7 _____

Persevere.

    James 1:2–3 _____

Practice contentment.

Philippians 4:12b _____

Psalms 73:2–3 _____

Proverbs 23:4–5 _____

1 Timothy 6:8 _____

Pursue generosity.

Proverbs 11:25 _____

Money Management Principles

Now that you've spent some time thinking about your spending habits, let's look at some basic money management principles. Keep these in mind as you work on your spending plan and as you revise the way you deal with your money.

1. ***There is an opportunity cost to consumption.*** Spending a dollar takes away multiple future dollars because the money you spent could have grown in an investment account. If you invest $1,000 at 10 percent for 25 years, it will grow to $10,835. When you spend the $1,000, you have lost all future growth. Financial maturity is being able to give up today's small pleasures for tomorrow's benefits.

2. ***Don't buy what you can't afford.*** Daily we are bombarded with advertising that identifies what we need to be better looking, happier, healthier, or to live like royalty. Pray continually for wisdom to be a discerning spender.

3. ***Commit to a slow, methodical savings program.*** A good savings program requires patience and self-discipline: "In the house of the wise are stores of choice food and oil, but a foolish man devours all he has" (Proverbs 21:20).

4. ***Money has time value.*** With compound interest, both the original investment and its interest earn more interest. The longer and earlier you get money working for you, the better off you are financially.

5. ***Money brings its own problems.*** Don't get caught up in believing that more money will solve all your problems. The danger is that the more money you possess, the more money can possess you. Use what you have wisely, and you'll be fine.

Monthly Spending Plan

The key to a spending plan is that total expenditures do not exceed spendable income. If, as you fill in the plan, your expenditures exceed your spendable income, don't panic. But realize that you have some work to do. Look first at your variable expenses to cut costs. Look through your plan to determine your spending habits, good and bad. Check that your plan gives priority to giving to the Lord and savings. Your monthly plan could look like this:

Category	Monthly Goal	Actual
Net Spendable Income	(use gross income minus taxes)	$
Savings	$	$
Housing	$	$
Utilities	$	$
Food	$	$
Car(s)	$	$
Insurance	$	$
Clothing	$	$
Medical	$	$
Debts	$	$
Entertainment	$	$
School/Child care	$	$
Other	$	$
Other	$	$
Other	$	$
Total Expenses	$	$
Net (Income minus expenses)	$	$
Surplus or (deficit)	$	$

How did you fare? Do you have a surplus or a deficit at the end of the month? If you have a deficit, now is the time to figure out where you can cut spending for next month. You may need to do it slowly. As with dieting, slowly and steadily makes for permanent weight loss, so with budgeting making changes slowly and surely will help make them permanent.

Avoid 10 Common Money Management Mistakes

Now that you're beginning to manage your money wisely, you'll want to be careful to avoid the pitfalls of money management.

1. *No spending plan.* Without a spending plan, you're likely to spend impulsively, use credit unwisely, and end up in unnecessary debt.

2. *No cash reserve.* A family should have between three and six months of expenses in reserve for use when emergencies arise.

3. *Too much use of credit.* (See chapter 5.) When handled wisely, credit can be good. Be careful not to use credit the "American way," to purchase something you really can't afford.

4. *Poor use of windfalls.* If you receive an extra sum of money through a bonus, inheritance, or tax refund, plan for its use just as you plan for other income. Before you treat yourself to a luxury item or exotic vacation, consider paying off debt, investing in education, or putting it aside in your cash reserve.

5. *No provision for large expenses.* Think about your future obligations. Planning for real estate taxes, house or life insurance premiums, or unexpected expenses (such as car repairs) is necessary if you expect to have the funds available.

6. *Underestimating the cost of ownership.* The more "things" you acquire the more you can expect to spend for upkeep and repair. Washers, dryers, microwaves, stereos, lawnmowers, stoves, refrigerators, and furnaces often require maintenance that costs money. For example, the expense of running and repairing a car is continual even if it's not consistent. Plan for these expenses.

7. *Spending leaks.* Impulse buying is a big problem for many people. Often the items purchased are small, but they will add up to a surprisingly large amount. Prevent improper spending by reducing the opportunities for spending. Only go to the malls or other stores when necessary, then go with a purpose and perhaps time constraints in mind.

8. *Careless shopping habits.* We live in a society that promotes everything imaginable, and we are told through advertisements our lives are not complete unless we own it all. Resist the pressure tactics of sales people and stick to your plans for what you'll buy and how much you'll spend.

9. *Not saving small amounts.* If all you can save is small amounts, don't get discouraged. Just as small expenditures add up, so do small savings.

10. *Can't-wait attitude.* Some people feel it is necessary to have it all and have it all right now. Young married couples, for example, might think they should have at the beginning of their life together what it took their parents 25 years to achieve. This is the time to develop patience and work on the "save now, buy later" principle.

Questions for Personal Reflection

Use the following questions to help you focus on your understanding of responsible money management.

1. What problems develop when you don't anticipate variable expenses? How can you improve your planning for variable expenses?

2. What responsible attitude does 1 Timothy 5:8 mandate? Managing money well is important to whom?

3. According to Proverbs 24:3–4, how do you become a responsible money manager so your rooms are filled with "rare and beautiful treasures"?

4. How large should a reserve or emergency fund be? How should you invest that fund?

5. How could your desire to keep up with the Joneses impact your spending plan?

6. What are some ways to eliminate impulse buying?

7. If your spending exceeds your income, what are some ways you can attempt to change the deficit to a surplus?

8. Explain the total impact of having money in savings earning compound interest versus interest charges compounding on a credit card balance.

9. What does Matthew 6:33 say you are to seek before wealth? How do you make that part of your financial planning?

10. List some things you can give up to reduce your spending.

Chapter 5

Controlling Debt

> God warns us about debt; the question is are we listening? This chapter shares some principles that will better enable us to control and eliminate debt.

The wicked borrow and do not repay, but the righteous give generously.
Psalm 37:21

Are there really only two certainties in life: death and taxes? Debt is likely a third. We live in a debt-filled society. Our government at all levels demonstrates financial mismanagement. Corporate America is burdened by debt. Each year, many well-known companies in America die because of their huge corporate debts. Individual debt is at record levels. According to "Hooked on Credit," *(USA Today,* May 28, 1996) 32 percent of those studied in a market survey had between five and nine credit cards.

Because of our borrowing habits, we are in debt overload. Most of us live on the installment plan, and borrowing is a part of life. Each year we waste tens of billions of dollars on excess interest payments, annual and late fees, and credit counseling.

What is debt? Simply stated, debt is anything we owe any person or institution. Often, debt is an obligation we take on because our desires exceed our ability to pay. With debt we can enjoy now and pay later.

Possibly the most widely violated principle in God's Word regarding money is our manner of borrowing and incurring debt. Scripture does not forbid us from borrowing money, but it does discourage us: "The rich rule over the poor, and the borrower is servant to the lender" (Proverbs 22:7). Despite God's warning, our dependence on debt continues to grow. For the proper purpose, borrowing can be advantageous, but most of the time borrowing can enslave a person to the lender.

To ensure your financial security, control your debt. If you must incur debt, do so wisely. In Matthew 7:24–29, Jesus speaks about the wise and foolish builders. If we handle our finances foolishly by using debt freely and loosely, we are building our financial houses on sand and creating false security. When problems such as job interruptions, overcommitment, sickness, and family expenses occur, a crash of the family finances is likely to take place if a family is deeply in debt. In contrast, when a family has only a small amount of debt or has not borrowed, its finances are more solid and can withstand greater economic pressures. Build your financial house on solid footing, not sinking sand.

The Bible and Debt

In Scripture God warns us to be cautious about debt. Perhaps debt is written about so much because God sees the need to warn us about the destructive power of debt and the damage it can cause. Debt creates bondage to the world and prevents us from allowing God to act as freely as He wants in our lives. Debt can hurt our personal witness and eat away at our souls: "Do not be a man who strikes hands in pledge or puts up security for debts; if you lack the means to pay, your very bed will be snatched from under you" (Proverbs 22:26–27).

"Let no debt remain outstanding, except the continuing debt to love one another, for he who loves his fellowman has fulfilled the law" (Romans 13:8). Does this verse imply that we should never borrow? Literally, it would be virtually impossible not to borrow money because each day in the month we owe on our electric, newspaper, phone, and water bills, and most of us owe on a home mortgage and automobile loan. We owe for services and goods we receive. The lesson is to pay off debt as soon as it is feasible.

Consequences of Debt

Excessive debt can devastate a family's financial future, create tension and chaos in the family, break up a marriage, and cause health problems. When debt is out of control, larger amounts of money need to be diverted to pay the interest and principal to creditors. Family goals are put in jeopardy. Debt problems grow because the loan's compounding interest works against the borrower. It is estimated that more than half of all Americans owe more than they own. This is a frightening statistic.

Money issues may monopolize a person's time, energy, and conversation. Things more important than money are no longer of interest or discussed. Prayer and Bible study may be ignored. We can't do what God wants us to do with our money because we already owe it to others. We are no longer free to use our God-given resources well. Our giving to God and others is reduced or stopped completely. Simply put, debt enslaves.

Your debt is too high if it causes anxiety and problems in your home or with your relationship with God. There is not an exact amount of debt that automatically predicts trouble for a family, but there are some percentages that can be used as guidelines. Any time you spend more than 20 percent of your net take-home income to pay off debt, you are spending too much. Families with good incomes or single people could possibly afford 20 percent, but it is unwise to be at that level. Most families with children should attempt to keep their debt service payments to 10 percent and preferably five percent or less of their net income.

Through debt we can lose our sense of reality. We live in homes that are owned in large part by a savings and loan or a bank. In our homes we have furniture owned by department stores for which we pay on installment plans. In our garages are cars owned by banks to which we pay on another plan. We come to believe we are on top of the world and can keep on borrowing. Using debt gives us an illusion that we have more money than we do. In reality, we are putting our futures in hock to finance them. Having too much debt imperils a family's ability to save for the future and prepare for emergencies.

Debt is both an opportunity loss and a financial loss. The more you pay in debt, the less you have to invest. Debt causes a depreciation of your asset base instead of allowing your goods and savings to create and appreciate in value. For example, if you pay $100 of interest expense monthly for 20 years, at 14 percent interest, you spend $130,117. If the $100 was invested in a growth mutual fund and returned an average of 12 percent annualized over the 20 years, it would return $98,926. The opportunity cost would be $229,043 of lost savings. Effective money management is getting money to work *for* you instead of *against* you.

Questions to Ask before Borrowing

Before taking on debt, ask yourself some basic questions. Be slow, deliberate, and cautious before you say yes to borrowing.

- Have I prayed about borrowing?

- Am I getting something of enough value when I borrow that it's worth the added obligation? Will the asset purchased appreciate in value?

- Will the borrowing allow me to give, save, and maintain my lifestyle?

- Does the borrowing fit my budget?

- Will the borrowing cause any tension or anxiety in my family?

- Is my borrowing showing any kind of improper pattern?

Let's say you've answered these questions and decided you can handle this debt. Do you know what interest rate you will be paying? Lenders don't give free lunches. Read the fine print and shop around for the best buys on credit. For example, a seven percent, five-year loan of $5,000, secured by a bank account, costs $99 a month, compared to $114 a month for an unsecured loan charging 13 percent. The lower rate loan will save $900 in the five-year period. Approximately 60 percent of credit card users have no idea what they paid last year in interest. If you can't avoid borrowing, at least be aware of what the charges are before you borrow.

If debt is unavoidable, you may want to explore the possibility of borrowing from relatives on a short-term basis. Your family may be able to help you through a temporary financial crunch. The interest you negotiate with your family may be more favorable than the 12 to 19 percent interest charges you may pay on credit card balances. To prevent the possibility of hard feelings or misunderstandings, any borrowing or lending between family members should be accompanied by written contracts.

If you have equity in a home, you may want to consider a home-equity loan because the interest expense is tax deductible. In addition, the interest rates charged are normally more reasonable than credit cards rates.

When Is Debt Acceptable?

All debt is not in the same category. A farmer may need to borrow as a course of his business. You may become unemployed, have an accident, be divorced, or be in other situations where debt, after much prayer and thought, is the only option. Improper debt is debt that is impulsive, discretionary, and unnecessary. You can't afford to mortgage your future for the desires of the present. Be sure you are incurring debt for good reasons and that you are able to pay off the debt quickly.

Appreciating Assets

If you can make a higher return on your investment than it costs to borrow, it makes sense to incur the debt. From an economic, comfort, and tax perspective, it is acceptable to borrow to purchase a home. In most locations, houses rise in value, creating an economic advantage to borrowing. It is also acceptable to borrow for education and for the car that takes you to work. These necessities are important enough to warrant debt. However, even this debt may be unreasonable if the house you purchase costs more than you are able to repay. Using debt for a vacation may, on the other hand, be unwise, because long after the fun and relaxation is over, bills still need to be paid.

A frequently asked question is "Is it better to rent or to buy a home?" Debt financing can work well with a home purchase. Appreciating real estate and the tax deductions for mortgage interest and real estate taxes may make buying economically wise. For example, if you purchase a $100,000 home:

Price of house	$100,000
Down payment	− 10,000
Mortgage amount	$90,000
Mortgage interest rate	× 8.5%
Interest expense	$7,650
Property tax	+ 1,000
Total expenses	$8,650
Income tax (28% Federal, 5% State)	× 33%
One year tax savings	$2,855
Annual estimated appreciation (3%)	+ $3,000
Total tax savings and appreciation	$5,855

Each year, the home owner pays mortgage and property taxes, but is able to reduce the cost of ownership by subtracting the income tax savings and any appreciation. In the above example, the owner would pay $7,650 in interest expense and $1,000 in property taxes, totaling $8,650, which is reduced by $5,855 in tax savings and appreciation, leaving a net cost of $2,795. Unless you can find a nice, comfortable apartment for less than $233 ($2,795 ÷ 12) per month, a house is the better value. Also, when the loan is paid off, the homeowner owns the home; the renter only has canceled checks. Since the interest expense will decline over the mortgage term, the net cost of home ownership will rise. Because of this, home ownership in later years may not be the better value.

The home-buying scenario discussed above may not be appropriate for many young, newly married couples. A house may be too much too soon. Besides a down payment which many newlyweds might not have, a home requires many expensive accessories. Young couples may budget for a home on two incomes and find their income is reduced when one parent stays home with the children. Since the maximum percentage of net income that should be spent on housing, insurance, and utilities is 40 percent, renting may be the better option for a period of time.

Consumable or Depreciating Assets

Ideally, debt should be used for investment in assets that appreciate in value. The worst use of debt is to purchase perishables such as gas, groceries, meals, etc. Once the item is consumed, the only thing remaining is debt. Any borrowing should be within your ability to pay without placing a strain on your budget.

You probably need a car for work. Incurring debt to purchase a car is reasonable. However, it is important to do some intelligent car buying because cars depreciate in value. A car loan may be reasonable, but a new car may not be. Studies have proven that it is less expensive to maintain a used car than to buy a new one. Resist the pressure to buy a new car that may not fit your budget. But remember that buying a used car doesn't have to take all the fun out of the purchase. Consider buying a program car (one that has been used as a rental or part of a company's fleet for a limited time). Program cars are usually still under warranty. It's not a brand new car, but it may feel more like it.

How Did I Get into Debt?

Debt may occur when there are circumstances beyond your control: accidents, illness, job loss, etc. However, most debt will occur and grow for one or more of these reasons:

Desire. Have you ever desired something you didn't need? Ever purchased something impulsively that you thought you had to have? God promises to give us all our needs but not all of our greeds. As a society we want things *now* and our culture says we deserve them. Because we desire more than we can afford, we purchase what we want on credit. That's when we can get into trouble. Luke 12:15 says, "Watch out! Be on your guard against all kinds of greed; a man's life does not consist in the abundance of his possessions." The key is not more, more, more. The key is trust, trust, trust! Trust in the Lord and resist what you don't need and can't afford.

Deception. When you really want something, you deceive yourself into believing you need it. Then you convince yourself you can't wait but need it *now*. Unfortunately, the store, bank, or lending agency will make borrowing very convenient—you can get almost anything for a few dollars down and several uneasy payments.

Ignorance. Even if you are smart and gifted and do well in your chosen career, you may be ignorant about debt. Few of us, if any, have taken classes on how to balance a checkbook or how to use credit cards correctly. Instead, we muddle through because we have little time to focus on finances. Proverbs 19:20 encourages us to "listen to advice and accept instruction, and in the end you will be wise." If you're thinking you could benefit from some instruction, look at a community center or community college for a class on basic money management techniques.

Poor Planning. Without budgets and goals, you are susceptible to impulse buying. The more long-range your perspective, the better decisions you will make today. If you have a long-range goal in mind, you are more likely to forego some immediate, unnecessary desires. Solomon tells us in Proverbs 14:15, "A simple man believes anything, but a prudent man gives thought to his steps." Planning will solve many poor spending habits.

Doubt. Because of our impatience and narrow-mindedness, we begin to doubt that God will provide. But He has His own timetable. And sometimes He says no.

Delay. When borrowing money, we often find it necessary to pay, at best, the minimum amount due on our credit card purchases. Of course, credit card companies prefer us to pay the minimum amount so they can charge more interest. By paying only the minimum, we pay interest on things purchased previously, and we pay immediate interest on any new purchases.

Mood Changes. Some people buy or spend money to get out of a depressed mood. There may not be a reason for the purchase, except that it helps emotionally. If you find yourself falling into that trap, find something else to do to cheer yourself up—go for a walk, call a friend, read a book, exercise, or, if you must go shopping, go without your wallet.[13]

Credit Card Rules

We are encouraged to take advantage of debt. Retail stores, telephone companies, car companies, airlines, etc., encourage us to develop credit with them. We are inundated with pre-approved credit card applications. All we need to do is supply a little information, sign an application, and instantly we have credit. Why do companies pressure us to borrow from them? Not because they are caring, thoughtful people but because they want to profit from our debt. Adhere to the following credit card rules to reduce spending and stop paying the high interest rates charged by credit card companies:

1. Establish a budget and use credit cards for items in the budget. Distinguish between what is a desire and what is actually needed. Restrict credit card purchases to what is needed.

2. Reduce the number of credit cards available for use to an absolute minimum. Fewer cards will reduce the temptation to spend. Just by having credit cards, you are vulnerable to buying more.

3. Most credit card companies give a 30-day grace period that enables you to pay off the debt without incurring interest expenses. At the end of that period, remit the full amount charged.

When the credit card bill is paid off regularly, the card is used only for convenience. To prevent any shocks at the end of the month, keep track of credit card purchases either using check registers or a financial software application.

4. If you are not able to pay off the card balances at the month's end, get rid of your cards and evaluate your spending habits.

Symptoms of Debt Problems

Before a debt crisis occurs, look for symptoms that will warn you of impending financial trouble:

▸ **Failure to pay off credit card balances**. Credit card companies encourage you to pay the minimum amount. If you borrow $1,000, the statement may say you only have to pay $50. The company doesn't want to be paid in full because it won't make as much. To avoid the debt obligation and high interest charges, pay off the balance monthly.

▸ **Failure to set aside emergency funds**. All of us have unexpected expenses. Problems of some sort are going to occur and things such as washers, dryers, cars, etc., are going to break down. Be prepared. Set aside emergency funds.

▸ **Failure to keep an adequate balance in the checking or savings account**. Does your checking account require a minimum balance for free checking? If so, keep that minimum balance and treat it as zero. Consider yourself overdrawn if you go below that balance. If you can't keep an adequate balance in your checking or savings account, you are becoming overextended.

▸ **Using savings to pay credit card bills**. Reserve savings for reaching your family's goals. Overspending can jeopardize your financial future.

▸ **Using advances from one credit card to pay off another**. This technique only postpones the problem.

▸ **Avoiding the mail, taking advances on pay checks, or being past due with basic living expenses such as rent or utilities.** These are symptoms of a serious debt management problem.

With or without debt problems, it is advisable to find out what your personal credit report says. If your report contains incorrect data, you have the opportunity to correct the difficulty or at least be prepared to deal with it at the time of borrowing. To obtain a free credit report, call Experiance (formerly TRW) at (800) 392-1122.

Advantages of Being Debt Free

Wouldn't it be wonderful not to have to make credit card payments, car payments, installment payments, or mortgage payments? If you were spending 5, 10, 15, or 20 percent of your budget on debt expense, that money is now freed for other purposes. This debt-free living can become more than a dream if you make it your number one financial goal. To be 100 percent debt free you need to make some plans and set some goals.

One-year goals

1. Reduce debt by 50 percent.
2. _____
3. _____

Five-year goals

1. Be totally debt free.
2. _____
3. _____

There are many advantages to being debt free. Add your own ideas to the following list.

1. **You can afford education.** Money that used to pay credit card interest charges and other interest expenses can be used for educational bills.

2. **You can save more for retirement.** After the school tuition expenses are paid, you are in good financial condition to save more for retirement. You may spend approximately one third of your life in retirement—will you have the resources to handle it?

3. **You will have less financial tension and stress.** Debt causes strife, worry, and anxiety. Having more things does not bring happiness. The debt obligation caused by buying those things will add pressure to your life.

4. **You will be able to take advantage of good investment opportunities.** Because you have additional funds, you can start letting your money grow in investments.

5. **You can increase your giving.** If you were previously tithing, you can go beyond the tithe. When you get out of debt, you have the opportunity to be more generous.

6. **You will be financially independent.** Money that was previously being spent on debt repayment can now accumulate and secure your financial future.

Credit Counseling

The Consumer Credit Counseling Service (CCCS) is a nonprofit organization affiliated with the National Foundation for Consumer Credit. The CCCS has more than a thousand offices throughout the United States. Its purpose is to provide one-on-one financial counseling, educational programs, and debt-management programs for families and individuals with financial problems. It is not a charity, a lending institution, or a governmental or legal agency. The CCCS is supported by contributions from credit unions, banks, finance companies, charities, and individuals. With their help, you can learn how to manage money and use credit more wisely. They can be reached at 8611 Second Avenue, Suite 100, Silver Spring, MD, 20910, or call 1-800-388-2227.

Another organization that offers credit counseling is Christian Credit Counselors, Inc., which has its headquarters in Casselberry, Florida. To set up a free Christian Counseling session, call 1-800-305-3328. Currently Christian Credit Counselors, Inc., has a limited number of offices, but they are expanding.

Getting Out of Debt

To get out of debt, you first need to understand how much in debt you are. Fill out the following worksheet, then read on to discover how to reduce those debts.

Mortgage	$
2nd mortgage (home equity loan)	$
Education	$
Credit card—Visa	$
Credit card—Master Card	$
Credit card—American Express	$
Credit card—Discover	$
Credit card—(other)	$
Credit card—(other)	$
Installment loan (1)	$
Installment loan (2)	$
Installment loan (3)	$
Car (1)	$
Car (2)	$

As you work to reduce your debt, be realistic. The borrowing probably took place over many years; it can't be reversed in one day. Following are some habits, practices, and attitudes that can help eliminate bad borrowing:

Conviction. If you are in debt, chances are you put yourself there. If you are overdue and overcommited, it's time to confess that you have been a poor money manager and have let your desires get the best of you. Pray daily that God will help make you a better steward of what He has entrusted to your care. You may want to pray the following prayer when you are paying your bills:

> Lord, as I begin this task of paying these obligations, give me a grateful heart. You have given me the health and the employment to be able to earn this money. Through the payment of these obligations, You are also at work providing for others. I confess that I have not been faithful in my financial stewardship this month. I ask for Your forgiveness. By the strength of Your Holy Spirit, grow in me an attitude of generosity to You and others. For all things, including this act of paying my obligations, I give You thanks for Yours is the kingdom and the power and the glory, forever and ever. Amen.

Commitment. Make a commitment that you will not be detoured from getting out of debt and staying away from borrowing. This is more than a desire, it's an attitude that nothing will stop you.

Lifestyle change. If your current spending habits and lifestyle put you in the debt fix, changes need to be made. The simple fact is that you can't afford to spend more than you earn, so prioritize your spending. The answer is not always making more money but spending it more wisely.

Cooperation. When borrowing involves a husband and wife, there needs to be a mutual agreement that both are willing to change.

Budget. A budget is often necessary to control borrowing. Review the sections on budgeting earlier in the book and take the time to create a budget. Then stick with it.

Counsel. By yourself you may not have the knowledge or commitment to change your borrowing habits. Seek out Christian help.

Review your status. You may need to stop contributions to your saving accounts or company 401(k) plans until your debt is paid off. It doesn't make sense to be receiving five percent, or even 10 percent on your investments, if you are paying 18 percent on your debts.[14]

Debt Reduction

Get out of debt in the following sequence:

1. *Eliminate all credit card debt.* A priority must be to pay off all credit cards. The full balance needs to be paid each month. In order to pay off credit card debt, consider postponing a vacation, reducing entertainment expenses, or delaying the purchase of a new car.

2. *Get out of car debt.* When you pay off a car loan, begin to set aside money monthly for the next car. A faithful savings program could enable you to pay cash for your next car purchase. If you can pay cash, you can take advantage of cash rebates. The cash rebate is often more advantageous than the special financing deals offered by the car companies.

3. *Start a mortgage prepayment program.* It can start with any extra monthly amount. Just $25 per month will reduce the principal owed, the interest expense, and duration of the loan.

Debt reduction or elimination (other than a home mortgage) is essential. To avoid financial chaos, control the amount of debt you incur. If you haven't been using credit to purchase things, you're off to a good start. If you have used credit excessively, now is the time to begin the arduous task of paying it off. If you're easily lured by purchasing offers such as "No money down, no payment for 90 days" turn and run! Such offers only encourage poor money management. Getting out of debt is no easy task but the benefits of being debt free are worth all the effort you can muster. Teach yourself to live by the maxim, "If I can't pay for it promptly, I won't buy it."

Questions for Personal Reflection

Use the following questions to help you focus on your understanding of debt and debt control.

1. How can debt hurt your personal witness?

2. What warning do you read in Proverbs 22:26–27?

3. Who does not repay debt (Psalm 37:21)?

4. What type of debt does God warn us about (Proverbs 17:18)?

5. When are we to repay debt (Proverbs 3:27–28)?

6. Does Romans 13:8 mean that no debt is to remain outstanding? Explain your answer.

7. How are we to lend to others (Luke 6:34–35)?

8. What rate of interest are we to charge our family on debt (Deuteronomy 23:19; Ezekiel 18:8)?

9. What does Proverbs 17:18 say about cosigning for debt?

10. God promises to give us our _____(Philippians 4:19), but not all our _____(Luke 12:15). It's up to us to control our desire for more things.

11. What are some forces in society that promote our desire for "things"?

12. What will happen to those who trust in their riches (Proverbs 11:28)?

13. Why do car and major appliance companies encourage and offer financing?

14. What does Proverbs 19:20 encourage?

15. What kind of example in debt control does our government provide?

16. What should we pray for according to Proverbs 30:7–9?

17. According to Proverbs 6:1–6, how important is it to free ourselves from debt?

Chapter 6

Prudent Investing

Wise investors will spend time and effort studying investment opportunities.

The blessing of the LORD brings wealth and He adds no trouble to it. Proverbs 10:22

Before developing investment strategies or examining investment principles, let's address two questions: "Why are we investing?" and "How will we use investment treasures?"

How Much to Invest

The amount of money you spend taking care of your family's needs will impact how much you can invest. If your lifestyle is out of control, the overspending robs God and limits opportunities to invest for the future. On the other hand, your family's needs must be met daily. The amount of money you can invest will depend on what you have left after your offerings and taking care of your personal needs. God wants you to multiply the money He gives you to invest, as shown in the parable of the talents. God gives you the privilege of choosing for yourself what you do with money.

Your investments play an important role in your ability to accumulate and compound the money God has given to you. Your individual circumstances determine what specific investments are appropriate for your situation. No one investment is right for everyone; the investments that are good for me may not be the best for you.

The following steps can help you understand how to prepare to invest:

1. Set financial goals.
2. Study investment vehicles.
3. Study financial markets and concepts.
4. Develop investment strategies.
5. Implement strategies.
6. Monitor investments.[15]

Investing begins by determining your financial goals that will determine what investments you should make. Below are factors that will influence your financial goal setting.

- ▶ investment time frame
- ▶ priorities
- ▶ investment funding potential
- ▶ return on investments
- ▶ age and career stage
- ▶ income needs
- ▶ risk tolerance

Begin studying for your investment opportunities by reading newsletters and magazines written to help investors. There are several hundred financial newsletters that are good sources of advice. The topics range from general economic information to detailed analysis of specific investments, such as stocks, bonds, real estate, and mutual funds.

Money Magazine is a good place to start. The material in *Money Magazine* is easy to understand and contains excellent facts about mutual funds and stock investments. Much of your success will be determined by how much you are willing to read and study. If you put only a small amount of time into acquiring an understanding of investment opportunities, your results will likely reflect those poor efforts. More helpful information can be found in the following publications:

- ▶ *The Wall Street Journal*
- ▶ *Investors Business Daily*
- ▶ *Kiplinger Personal Finance*
- ▶ *Weisenburger Investment*
- ▶ *Morningstar Fund Value*
- ▶ *Standard and Poor's Analysis*
- ▶ *Barrons Weekly*

Good financial information is not limited to these resources, but they are excellent publications.

For individual stock selections, you may want to review *Value Line Investment Survey,* which can be found in most libraries. You can subscribe to *Value Line* by calling 1-800-833-0046. The stocks *Value Line* recommends for purchase are given a "1" rating; stocks they recommend selling a "5." Each company is thoroughly researched regarding information on sales, profits, profit margins, debts, tax ratios, price/earning ratios, and earning projections.

Financial planners and stockbrokers are available to you as consultants. Most people in this field are commissioned salespeople so the products they recommend will generate a commission.

As a former stockbroker, I know the public perception of stockbrokers is mixed. Some people have the same attitude about stockbrokers they do about politicians, divorce lawyers, or used-car salesmen. Just as there are excellent and honest politicians, divorce lawyers, and used-car salesmen, there are excellent stockbrokers. A good stockbroker can offer invaluable assistance to the novice as well as to the experienced investor.

Before doing business with a stockbroker research his or her background, including experience, investment philosophy, references, and any history of disciplinary action. In addition to finding out information about the broker, ask about the firm he or she represents. Commission rates and availability of products will vary among firms so they should be compared as well.

Financial planners usually work on a fee basis rather than on commission. If you feel it's necessary to hire professional help and can afford it, a fee-based planner offers a possible advantage because there will be no conflict of interest. The planner does not receive a commission on investment products, so he or she does not have an incentive to direct you into high-commission investments.

Identifying Investment Objectives

You may be saying, "I have no idea where to invest my money." Don't worry—you're not alone. To begin, set one or two specific financial goals. Picture yourself where you want to be 5, 10, or 20 years down the road. After you've set your goals, you can develop the best route to get there.

Your objectives, derived from the goals you've developed, will likely be affected by your risk tolerance, age, and stage in life. Ask yourself, "What are some important factors affecting my investment decision?" A possible answer is: "I want my investments to give me a good return." However, that response leaves questions about what kind of return, how involved you want to be, or what risks you are willing to take.

Let's look at investment objectives. They relate to the attributes you determined you need in your investments. Investment objectives are:

- safety and preservation of invested dollars
- hedge against inflation
- tax-free return
- current income
- appreciation/growth
- liquidity of the investment
- ease of management
- ability to add or withdraw
- diversification

If you don't define your objectives, you may be disappointed in your investment results. No single investment can satisfy all of your objectives. Typically an investor will select an appropriate mix of investments.

Investment Options

In grandpa's day, the family savings were often tucked under a mattress, hidden in the flour bowl, or stuffed in a hole. Today, investment options are quite extensive. Your investment choices can be safe or risky, short- or long-term, income or growth, U. S. or overseas, simple or complex. For many people, the choices are too many. They choose not to invest because there are so many choices and decisions to make they become confused and give up. If that sounds like you, stick with it. Do it a little at a time until you feel comfortable with all the information.

Perhaps a good place to start is with the amount of risk you're willing to take. The degree of risk is a major component in choosing among investment alternatives. Investment results can be greatly affected by a small percentage change on the return from your investment. The following illustration points out the importance of getting the best return possible on your investments.

Impact of 2% on a $10,000 investment

	10 years	20 years	30 years
10% return	$25,937	$67,275	$174,494
12% return	$31,058	$96,463	$299,599

No Risk. The comfort levels of some individuals might influence them to make a no-risk investment, such as short-term insured bank certificates of deposit (CDS) or short-term U. S. treasury bills. After inflation and taxes, there is very little return with these investments, but the principal is not at risk. It's not wise to take more risk than is absolutely necessary, but the phrase "no risk, no return" would apply to short-term CDS and short-term treasury bills. If you maintain investments in a bank, be sure the bank is insured by the Federal Deposit Insurance Corporation (FDIC). Not all banks provide the same rate of return, so shop around for the best rates and services.

Another option for safe money is U. S. Savings Bonds. This investment is backed by the U. S. Government because you are actually loaning money to the government. You can purchase these bonds at most banks, and there are no fees to purchase them. The EE bonds are bought at a discount (50 percent of face value), and they mature at face value. During the holding period, there is no current taxation but there is a tax consequence when you withdraw the money. For the rate on bonds held five years or more call 1-800-USBONDS.

Low Risk. Income-oriented investments, such as high quality corporate bonds, municipal bonds (tax-free bonds), and highly rated income stocks, are very low in risk. Highly rated corporate and municipal bonds have very little risk of default as do blue chip utility stocks. The prices of bonds are affected by interest rates. A change in the prevailing interest rates will cause bond prices to fluctuate. A rise in interest rates by the Federal Reserve will cause bond prices to decline, which would cause a temporary reduction in principal. Unless a default occurs, bonds will mature at face value.

The money market mutual fund is a vehicle that allows a decent rate of return, liquidity, and extremely low risk. Money market mutual funds normally offer a better return than daily passbook savings at banks. Many funds also allow check-writing privileges. One drawback of the money market mutual fund is the amount of money needed to start the fund.

Moderate risk. The volatility of the stock market underscores the potential risk of stocks, but over the past 70 years the equity markets have provided investors with average annual double-digit returns. For moderate business or market risk, you need a well-diversified portfolio.

For the most part, real estate is also a moderate risk investment. Ordinarily, real estate increases in value with inflation, but there are no guarantees. Investment in real estate is more difficult than stocks and bonds because of the need for larger amounts of money and the difficulty in selling when you want to have access to your money. In addition to less liquidity, real estate is more expensive to buy and sell, and it is subject to local market conditions.

If you invest in real estate, you must be willing to spend time looking at properties, collecting rent checks, and providing maintenance. As an investment it is all worthwhile, if the real estate appreciates.

High risk. A high-risk investment is a speculative investment that is made in the hope of earning a large profit in a short time. Commodity futures and precious metals are examples of high risk investments. The volatility of commodity futures is much greater than stocks. Because you can lose more money than you invest in commodities, this type of investment for speculators should be reserved for high risk takers. This could be the ultimate high risk/high reward investment. With the greater risk of loss also comes the potential greater reward of success. Investors need to understand the risk and reward potentials. Gemstones, coins, stamps, and antiques are high risk investments, but the risk can be reduced if you are informed and deal with reputable dealers.

Diligent Investing

Study the following Scripture references to deepen your understanding of biblical investing principles.

Develop a God-pleasing plan.

Proverbs 14:15 _____

Proverbs 16:3 _____

Proverbs 3:5 _____

Discuss your plans with your family and trusted financial advisor.

Proverbs 15:22 _____

Proverbs 19:20 _____

Devote time to understanding investments, concepts, and strategies.

Proverbs 23:23 _____

Proverbs 15:14 _____

Proverbs 24:3–4 _____

Proverbs 16:16 _____

Proverbs 10:14 _____

Proverbs 13:14 _____

Discount get-rich schemes.

Proverbs 16:13 _____

Proverbs 13:11 _____

Psalm 37:7 _____

Proverbs 10:2 _____

Proverbs 12:11 _____

Proverbs 28:20 _____

Determine timing strategies (asset allocation).

Proverbs 6:6–8 _____

Decline to speculate.

Proverbs 21:29 _____

Proverbs 27:12 _____

Discipline yourself.

Proverbs 10:4–5 _____

Proverbs 13:4 _____

Proverbs 14:23 _____

Proverbs 21:5 _____

Diversify your investments.

Matthew 25:21 _____

Proverbs 24:3–4 _____

Ecclesiastes 4:9; 11:2 _____

Determine your net after-tax return.

Matthew 22:21 _____

Romans 13:6–7 _____

Don't co-sign.

Proverbs 11:15 _____

Exodus 22:26 _____

Proverbs 22:26 _____

Proverbs 17:18 _____

Psalm 109:11 _____

Stock Investing Can Be Profitable

When you buy stock in a corporation, you become a shareholder in the company. When a company wants to raise capital, it can borrow money from a bank, or it can issue stocks or bonds to the public. As a part owner of the business, you benefit from increased earnings in two ways: (1) dividends and (2) appreciation in the value of the stock. Your proof of ownership is a stock certificate issued in your name, identifying the number of shares you own.

To keep pace with inflation and to provide above-average growth potential, many investors should consider investing some of their money in stocks. How successful can investing in stocks be? If an investor bought Federal Express shares when they were initially sold for $3 to the general public in 1978, within 10 years he would have received 1800 percent. An investment of $1,000 in Ford Motor Company in 1912 would have grown to $12 million by 1950. With IBM, $2,000 grew to $700,000 in 40 years.

Success stories, such as Federal Express, Ford, and IBM happen, but are not everyday experiences. In comparison to bank certificates of deposit, bonds, real estate, and precious metals, stocks have, over the past four decades, provided investors with a better return. Since 1926, the stock market has returned an average per year in excess of 10 percent, including the market crashes of 1929 and 1987. A beginning investor may want to consider investing in industry-leading companies and possibly basic industry groups, such as food or beverage. It would also be advisable to select more than one company and more than one industry. Stocks listed on the New York or American stock exchange give added protection because of the size of the company and your ability to buy or sell.

Types of Stocks

As you look at the stock quotes in the paper, you can see thousands of stocks that are actively traded. Most of them can be classified as blue-chip, income, growth, cyclical, special situation, or preferred.

Blue-chip stocks. A blue-chip stock is a safe investment that is attractive to conservative investors. Stocks of companies are called blue-chip if they have a history of good earnings, have been leaders in their industry, and have a good earnings potential. General Motors, Eastman Kodak, Coca-Cola, and General Electric are examples of companies with blue-chip stocks.

Income stocks. An income stock pays higher than average dividends. Income stocks are more about income potential than growth. Your local electric and gas utility companies are examples of income-producing stocks. Many utility companies pay a current dividend of about 6 percent and also increase the return to investors fairly often, if not yearly. Stocks of public utility companies have consistently been sound, high-yielding investments. Utilities are also appealing because of their dividend reinvestment plans, which enable investors to accumulate more shares.

Growth stocks. These are stocks of companies whose earnings have increased at an above-average rate. The companies normally pay a small dividend to the stockholders but reinvest most of the earnings into the company.

Cyclical stocks. As the general economy goes through expansions and contractions, so do many companies in cyclical industries. As a Detroit resident, I see firsthand the adding and releasing of auto industry employees as the production of cars increases or decreases. When the big three car companies add employees to fill the demand for new cars, the profits are normally rising, which should move their stock prices higher.

Special situation stocks. The most speculative but potentially the most profitable stock investment is the special situation stock. It normally involves a new industry or a new product that could be a sales bonanza or a total failure, causing a stock investment to skyrocket or fall apart.

Preferred stocks. Preferred stocks do not participate in the added growth in profits of a company, but do receive a higher fixed dividend. If you are interested in higher income than common stocks or most banks pay, you may want to consider preferred stock shares.

Dividend Reinvestment Plans. To provide additional potential for growth in your stock investments, you might reinvest the cash dividends in additional shares. If you own shares, many companies will give investors the option to invest their dividends into more shares, often with no commission charges. Through dividend reinvestment plans you have the opportunity to bypass stockbrokers.

Finding the Price of Stocks

Most major newspapers quote the prices from the New York Stock Exchange. Let's look at Ford Motor Company as it was shown in *USA Today* on January 30, 1997.

High	Low	Stock	Div	Yld	PE	Sales (00)	Last	Chg
37⅛	28¾	Ford M	1.54	4.7	11	76558	37⅞	--

High-Low: The highest and lowest price a stock traded during the last 52-week period.

Stock: Name of the company or stock (abbreviated).

Div: The dividend—the amount of money the company pays per share in a year.

Yld: The percentage yield—determined by dividing the dividend amount by the current price of a stock.

PE: The price/earnings ratio—the price of the stock today divided by the current earnings per share of the company.

Sales: The number of shares of stock in hundreds that changed hands during the day of trading.

Last: The closing price on the given day of trading.

Chg: The change in stock price from the preceding day of trading.

Analyzing Stocks

Simply stated, to do well in the stock market, buy low and sell high. The two disciplines in analyzing stock investments that help you know when to buy and sell are technical and fundamental analysis.

Technical analysis. A technical analysis is not concerned with company debt, profit margins, taxes, or management. Rather, the technician is interested in past stock price movement to predict future price changes. The thought is that by charting a stock's price, the technical analysis will help you know what stocks to buy and when to sell.

Fundamental analysis. The fundamental approach looks at the company's internal factors and operations, including the track record of the company or management, research and development, cost of production, the price/earning ratio, debt ratio, profit margin ratio, growth in earnings per share, etc. A key analysis is the price/earning ratio, which is calculated by dividing the current price by the earnings per share for the past year. If XYZ Company normally trades on the exchange at 10 times earnings (price divided by earnings per share) but dips to eight times earnings, it may represent a buying opportunity. If the earnings were $3 per share with a PE (price/earnings ratio) of 12, the stock would sell at \$36. But with a PE of 8, the stock would trade at \$24 (8 × 3). The PE ratio can help determine if a stock is under- or overpriced. One source from which to gather information about a company is the *Value Line Investment Survey*.[16]

How do you choose stocks? The simplest and most basic investment strategy for you as a consumer is to look around you at the products and services you really enjoy. If you benefit from and appreciate certain merchandise, it's likely others do as well. The next step is to check the company that manufactures and sells those items.

Stock Averages

The Dow Jones Industrial Average (DJIA), dating back to 1896, is the most commonly quoted average in the world. It is also the oldest. It is a small average because it is made up of only 30 blue-chip stocks. The 30 companies are household names, such as AT&T, Exxon, General Electric, Coca-Cola, IBM, General Motors, Johnson & Johnson, and Wal-Mart.

When the market is reported up or down on radio or television, most reports are referring to the Dow Jones Industrial Average. These 30 established companies comprise only a small percentage of value on the New York Stock Exchange, but they indicate very well the overall direction of the market. A prolonged upward movement in the DJIA indicates a bull market, and a downward direction indicates a bear market.

Investing in Stocks through Mutual Funds

A mutual fund is an investment company owned by shareholders that makes investments on behalf of individuals. Whether you invest a few dollars or several thousand, your investments are pooled with other investors. Due to the success of mutual fund investments, you can now select from more than 3,000 different mutual fund companies. The kinds of mutual funds range from open-end to closed-end funds; short-term, long-term, high-yield, taxable and tax-exempt, insured and uninsured income funds; there are equity funds that include balanced, growth, growth and income, large/small company, asset allocation, sector, global, international index funds, plus many more. The investment philosophy of investment managers will range from very conservative to extremely risky. Select a fund that matches your personal investment philosophies. Investing in a mutual fund simply means buying shares of the fund. The fund you purchase is in the business of investing in securities, and the value of the shares you buy is determined by the securities owned by the fund.

Advantages of Mutual Funds

▸ **Professionally managed.** Mutual fund assets are managed by professional managers.

▸ **Diversification.** Mutual fund investments are pooled with other investors. Money fund managers can invest in hundreds of different companies, providing a diversified portfolio. This diversification reduces the risk because the investment is spread out over so many different equities. The more stocks you own, the less impact a poor stock selection has on the total investment.

▸ **Reinvestment.** You can contribute additional money to mutual funds every month and also

100

have the income and capital gains reinvested. The reinvestment opportunity allows for growth by accumulating additional shares of the fund. A reinvestment plan also incorporates the dollar cost averaging concept, which is described later in this chapter.

- ▸ **Withdrawals.** Mutual funds can be set up to send out a check each month.

- ▸ **Choice of investment objectives.** Mutual funds offer a wide variety of investment choices that let you match your needs and goals with the objectives of the funds. Fund objectives may be income, tax-free income, conservative growth, aggressive growth, international investing, etc.

- ▸ **Liquid.** Mutual funds can be sold quickly and normally without any redemption charge.

- ▸ **Easy to buy.** Mutual funds are easy to buy. Funds are either sold by a broker or sold directly to the public through advertising.

Mutual Fund Facts

- ▸ **Load vs. No-Load.** As an investor, when you pay an initial commission charge on your mutual fund purchase, you are buying a loaded fund. There are also back-end loaded funds available that allow you to pay the commission charge only if you sell the fund before a stated length of time. You can also buy funds with no commission charges, which are referred to as no-load funds. Mutual funds with a commission charge are sold through commission brokers. All mutual funds charge an annual management fee of approximately one percent. Some mutual funds are sold as 12b-1 funds (back-end surrender charges), which causes an investor to pay a commission if the fund is sold within six years after the initial purchase. All fees charged by a fund are described in the prospectus.

- ▸ **Open-end Fund.** Open-end mutual fund investment companies continually issue new shares for sale to the public and redeem shares at the request of the investors. An open-end fund puts no limit on the number of shares that can be issued. Both the number of shares and the funds value are related to the value of the securities the fund holds. The price reported is the Net Asset Value (NAV), which is determined by the total market value of all the stocks owned by a fund divided by the number of shares.

- ▸ **Closed-end Fund.** Funds that own a diversified stock or bond portfolio that do not offer additional shares to the public are called closed-end funds. Only a certain number of shares are available to investors. Closed-end funds trade on exchanges and do not sell at net asset value but rather fluctuate based on supply and demand. Because of the ease of buying and selling, as well as the investment results over the past several years, mutual fund sales are increasing and more households than ever own funds. Mutual funds can fit almost everywhere in investment portfolios because funds are offered from low risk to high risk, income to growth.

Investing in Bonds

Corporate bonds are a source of financing for corporations in the same way government bonds provide funds for the U. S. Treasury. Bonds are a debt obligation of the entity offering the bond.

With bonds, investors make loans to governments or corporations. The investor invests in the bonds, expecting to receive interest payments and the return of his principal.

Why would you be interested in buying bonds versus stocks? Since bonds offer a higher and more dependable level of current income and are less volatile than stocks, many investors are interested in bonds. Because bonds pay a set amount of interest at set time periods, they are referred to as fixed-income assets.

Bonds typically pay interest semiannually. If you purchase an eight percent XYZ bond with a $10,000 par value, you will receive $400 every six months until the bond matures.

Two risks associated with bonds are (1) default—the company or government may be unable to continue paying the interest as well as return the principal; (2) changing interest rates in the economy affect the trading price of the bond. If interest rates trend higher in the U.S. economy, the prices of existing bonds will decline causing a loss for the investor if the bond needs to be sold. Bond mutual funds are available to investors who can purchase professionally managed, diversified bond funds. Most of these funds pay a monthly income. You can sell your bond funds before maturity in the secondary market through a stockbroker, but you may not receive what you initially paid.

Bond rating services, such as Moody's and Standard & Poor's, can help you determine the quality and safety of bonds. The highest rating is a "AAA" and the lowest is a "D" rating. Any rating of "BBB" or higher is considered investment grade.

Proper Allocation of Investment Options

When you know your objectives and understand how you can use bank CDs, stocks, bonds, mutual funds, or real estate to accomplish those objectives, you can develop, if funds are available, a portfolio that uses several different investments. The question is how much should you allocate to these different investment choices? The way you divide up your money among different investment choices is called asset allocation. It is very prudent to diversify using some fixed-income investments, some growth investments, some long- and short-term bonds. The overall mix of assets can be more important than individual selection of stocks, bonds, or other investments. It is also important to adjust your allocation proportions as your stage in life changes. If you visited more than one financial planner who carefully looked at your financial situation, you would likely get different asset allocation recommendations. There is no textbook answer. Your age, needs, and risk tolerances will help determine a reasonable investment mix.

Consider the following example of an asset allocation recommendation as you think about your own asset allocation possibilities:

Age	Life Cycle	Major Needs	Possible Investment Allocation
20s	*Family formation*; starting out—mastering the financial basics	Educational debt, car, home, furnishings, wardrobe, financial protection	75% Growth 5% Income 20 % Money Market
30s	*Family growth*; juggling family finances and growth	Children expenses, reserve fund, college expenses, education fund, retirement savings	70% Growth 15% Income 15% Money Market
40s	*Mid years*; greatest earning power years	Saving for college, retirement, tax and estate planning, home sale/relocation, pay off all debt	65% Growth 20% Income 15% Money Market
50s	*Preretirement*; prepare now for your later years	Retirement, positioning, retirement savings, changing lifestyle	60% Growth 30% Income 10% Money Market
60s	*Retirement*; living well in retirement	Changed lifestyle, volunteer service, travel, philanthropy	45% Growth 45% Income 10% Money Market

Tax-free vs. Taxable Income

An important maxim for investors is: "It's not what you make but what you keep that counts." Taxes certainly reduce your net after-tax return on most investments. Current tax laws allow schools, cities, counties, state projects, and nonprofit organizations to be funded by tax-free municipal bonds. This source of funding allows those entities to pay less interest, which investors willingly receive because they don't have to pay federal income tax on interest earned on municipal obligations. In addition, most states do not tax municipal income for bonds issued in their states.

You may have to decide whether to invest in a taxable investment at a given rate or in a tax-free investment. For example, if you are in the 28 percent tax bracket, should you invest in a 7 percent corporate bond or a 5.5 percent municipal bond when both bonds have the same maturity? To answer that question, you need to know what tax-free yield is equal to a 7 percent taxable yield for your income tax rate. To calculate the equivalent tax-free yield, which equals a taxable rate of income, use the following formula:

$$(1 - \text{tax bracket rate}) \times (\text{taxable yield}) = \text{equivalent tax-free yield}$$

Using the corporate bond rate as the taxable yield, the formula becomes:

$$(1 - .28) \times .07 = X$$

$$.72 \times .07 = 5.04$$

Therefore a 5.04 percent tax-free yield is equal to a 7 percent taxable rate for a person in a 28 percent tax bracket. After you pay your 28 percent taxes on a 7 percent investment, you are receiving a 5.04 percent net return. In the example, the 5.5 percent municipal bond would provide a better after-tax return than the corporate bond, indicating the municipal bond is the best choice.

The Taxable Equivalent Advantage

Taxable Equivalent Yield. (Interest rate needed on a tax-free investment to equal a taxable return.)

Tax-free Yield	28% Tax Bracket	31% Tax Bracket
5.0%	6.94%	7.25%
5.5%	7.64%	7.97%
6.0%	8.33%	8.7%[17]

Municipal bonds have been referred to as the second safest investment next to U.S. government bonds. The safety reference certainly applies to those bonds backed by general obligation tax powers of cities, counties, or state governments. Tax-free bonds backed by the revenue from a nonprofit hospital or a city ball park, etc., will likely not be of the same quality. Some municipal bonds are issued with insurance of principal by an outside insurance company.

Individual municipal bonds, normally sold in increments of $5,000, may be purchased from brokerage firms. Municipal bonds in a tax-free mutual bond fund can be purchased in smaller increments.

Not tax-free, but tax-deferred. For tax-deferred investments, invest in annuities and/or in IRAs. The investments will grow tax-free until the income is withdrawn. If you have a period of time in which the growth and interest are compounding and not diminished by taxes, your investments can increase at a faster rate.

To illustrate the benefits of tax-deferred compounding, let's assume you have $10,000 to invest for a period of 20 years at 8 percent. If you pay taxes yearly on one investment in a 28 percent tax bracket, you will have $30,650. In a second investment, if you invest the same $10,000 for 20 years but do not pay taxes on the earnings, your investment will grow to $46,610. There are obvious advantages to deferring the taxes as long as possible.

Because of these advantages, it is wise to invest as much as you can afford into 401(k) and

403(b) plans as well as IRAs. These retirement plans provide some of the best opportunities you have of getting your money to grow. But be aware of the 10 percent federal penalty if you withdraw money from qualified retirement plans before age 59½. 401(k) and 403(b) contributions will, in addition, reduce your income tax expense the year the investments are made.

Advantages of Tax-deferred Investments

$1,000 at 6 percent tax-deferred versus $1,000 at 6 percent taxes at 28 percent:

	10 years	20 years	30 years
Tax-deferred	$1,791	$3,207	$5,743
Taxable	$1,379	$1,892	$2,642

Diversification

It is important to spread your risk across a number of different investments. Diversification is the best strategy for reducing the risk and increasing the return. The stock market crash of 1987 illustrates the value of diversification. If all your investments were in growth stocks, you would likely have been panic stricken. By diversifying, you reduce your risk versus a single stock or bond. Put your eggs in more than one basket.

Having a variety of investments can also reduce the volatility of what you own. If you own both U.S. and international stocks, one market might be doing well while the other is not. Owning several stocks in different industries can also give a stabilizing effect to your portfolio. Many investors balance their investments among stocks, bonds, and money market funds to reduce the volatility.

Earlier in this chapter, it was noted that an advantage of mutual fund investing is the fund's ability to help you diversify. You can diversify further by investing in more than one mutual fund, especially with the purpose of using funds for different objectives.

Dollar Cost Averaging

Dollar cost averaging works on the premise that you invest a fixed dollar amount in stocks or mutual funds regularly. By investing regularly you could be buying additional shares when the price is lower. Dollar cost averaging works well with 401(k) or 403(b) plans when regular contributions are being made. The dollar cost averaging method helps to cushion stock market fluctuations.

Here's how it works: Assume a shareholder invests $100 every other month over a year's time. The share price of the fund varies between $10 and $5 during this period. The account would look like this:

Price	Shares Purchased
$10	10.0
$8	12.5
$6	16.7
$5	20.0
$6	16.7
$8	12.5

Total shares purchased:	88.40
Average cost/share:	$ 6.79
Average price/share:	$ 7.17
Value of account if sold:	$707.20

If the price remained at $10 throughout the year, the shareholder would have accumulated only 60 shares that, in turn, would have been sold for $600. The decline in share price actually worked to the shareholder's advantage when dollar cost averaging was employed because the value at the end was $707.20. Of course, dollar cost averaging can't protect an investor in a continuously declining market.[18]

Common Investment Mistakes

There are many mistakes investors can make. Here are six to watch for:

1. *Following the Crowd.* This process has been referred to as the "herd instinct." When everyone else buys, you buy. When everyone else sells, you sell. You assume the crowd is right. So if selling begins, you don't want to be the last fool. You sell too. If the market is going higher and people are buying, you get greedy and don't want to be left behind; therefore, you buy too. Don't let the crowd determine your financial future. Remember, good investment strategies vary from investor to investor. What's good for one isn't necessarily good for another.

2. *Avoiding Risk.* If you are never willing to take any risk, your investment return probably won't be much better than the rate of inflation. The key is "calculated risk" not "foolish risk." Many investors are too conservative and need to put some money into stocks.

3. *Acting on a "Hot Tip."* Rarely is money made on a "hot tip." Good investments are made through careful analysis and hard work.

4. *Failing to Carry Through on Your Determination to Save.* If you don't save, you can't invest. The key is to save often and much.

106

5. *Failing to Monitor Your Investment's Performance.* Once you start investing, you need to monitor and evaluate the performance your investments are achieving. Keeping good records is essential.

6. *Buying into a Financial Scam.* Be careful of your potential gullibility to believe all you hear. It may be necessary to discount what you hear and be able to say no.[19]

Your investment success can be the determining factor in whether you accomplish your financial goals. You work hard to earn your money—take the necessary steps to achieve a good return on your investments. But keep your focus on the reason for your investments: good stewardship of the gifts God has given you.

Questions for Personal Reflection

Use the following questions to help you focus on your understanding of wise investing.

1. What does Matthew 6:19 say about earthly treasures?

2. What does Matthew 6:24 say about the choices we must make?

3. What happens to those who put their wealth before God (Proverbs 28:20)?

4. What are the consequences for not diligently managing and investing money (Proverbs 24:33–34)?

5. Where does God want some of our treasures to go (Proverbs 3:27; Acts 2:45)?

6. What do we read regarding the wise in Proverbs 21:20?

7. What does God say about planning (Proverbs 14:15; 16:3)?

8. How important is it for us to seek knowledge and wisdom in our investing (Proverbs 10:14; 15:14; 16:16; 23:23; 24:3-4)?

9. What warnings are we given about get-rich schemes (Proverbs 10:2; 12:11; 13:11, Psalm 37:7)?

10. What is said about future financial planning (Proverbs 21:29; 27:12)?

11. How important are effort and discipline in our financial activities (Proverbs 14:23; 21:5)?

12. Investing money only for the sake of having more money isn't wise stewardship. What does Scripture say about hoarding money (Proverbs 11:26; James 5:3; Ecclesiastes 5:13)?

Chapter 7

Retirement Planning

People are living longer and retiring earlier. It's a real challenge to acquire enough money to retire comfortably. But with preparation, retirement can provide a greater opportunity for Christian service.

"For I know the plans I have for you," declares the LORD, "plans to prosper you and not to harm you, plans to give you a hope and a future."
Jeremiah 29:11

It used to be that people retired at 65 and most died by 72, which allowed only a few short retirement years. That is no longer the case. Today many of us will retire at 55 or 60 and, because of advances in medicine, many of us will live to 85 or 90 or longer. Instead of a few years of retirement, many of us will experience 30 or more years of life after work.

Do you have the resources to spend up to a third of your life in retirement? During your working years you have the challenge to be saving for retirement, so the sooner you start planning and saving, the better prepared you'll be. Retirement can be the time when you enjoy the fruits of your labors or, if you aren't prepared, it can plunge you into boredom, depression, and even despair. With preparation retirement can be a fun, fulfilling time.

Certainly retirement ranks high among life's major milestones—along with college, starting a job, marriage, and parenthood. But retirement means different things to different people. Some continue being active in the same profession; others begin a new career altogether. Still others do as little as possible, travel, or pursue their hobbies and interests. In retirement you can give time to lifelong interests or even start a part-time business. But there are some things you should attempt to accomplish financially before you retire so you can live more comfortably when retirement comes. Inadequately funding your retirement could prevent you from doing the things in your golden years that you've looked forward to, so it is a good idea to plan wisely for retirement. But it may not be easy. Look at some of the problems our country is facing:

- The Social Security system's future is in question.

- Medicare is projected to be broke by 2001.

- Medical costs have been increasing faster than inflation.

- Taxes at the national and local levels are increasing.

- Inflation is taking its bite out of our purchasing power.

Planning for an enjoyable retirement is a challenge, but you can make it happen.

Is Retirement Biblical?

Retirement is a modern-day phenomenon. Today we believe that at some point in our lives we can stop working and enjoy a different lifestyle to the fullest. How does that fit with being a Christian? Scripture does not refer to retirement, so how should we use it? The time could be used to help build God's kingdom. If you choose to increase your level of volunteer work in the church, you would greatly benefit the church through your support, wisdom, and experience. However, if you use your time simply to eat, drink, and be merry, you are being a poor steward of God's gifts.[20]

The dictionary defines *retire* as "to withdraw from action, or retreat." Retirement can certainly allow time for traveling, reading, golfing, fishing, and other interests; the key seems to be moderation—finding a balance between enjoying yourself and your family and still having time to be of service to others.

Larry Burkett, in his book *Preparing for Retirement*, refers to a study done at Harvard University that looked at 65-year-old male graduates: 100 men who had retired and 100 who had not. At age 75, seven out of eight of the retirees had died, while seven out of eight of the nonretirees were still alive and well. Obviously some of the men who retired may have done so because of health reasons. But that is not the only explanation for the difference. Besides providing needed or extra income, there appears to be an even greater reason to work—living longer![21]

So does that mean you have to stay in your current job until you're over 75? Certainly not. They key, again, is planning ahead. The preretirement challenge is to save enough during the working years so that during retirement you have freedom to serve. Without an early savings plan, you may not have the time in retirement to serve others through the church; you may need to spend much of your time just making a living.

Without an adequate savings plan you may find yourself lowering your standard of living or working longer than you had expected. Some folks do such a good job of preparing financially for retirement that they are in the opposite, enviable situation: having a surplus of money that will never be used. To avoid either scenario, work for a proper balance between your current and future needs, and the needs of others. God wants us to live comfortably, but He may have additional purposes for a large savings account: "A generous man will himself be blessed, for he shares his food with the poor" (Proverbs 22:9).

Retiring Earlier

The notion of retirement is changing. The days of a person working for the same company for 35–40 years and building up a big pension are all but disappearing. Retiring exactly at age 65, for many of us, is no longer the dream. Because of our greater mobility, corporate downsizing and restructuring, our careers aren't so predictable nor is the beginning of our retirement. Retirement has become another stage of life that comes after we've raised our children and we've finished what we wanted to do.

If you don't want to work during retirement, you will need to spend a great deal of effort and planning before retirement. There are many hindrances to a comfortable retirement including:

▸ no goal setting or too little planning

▸ lack of disciplined saving

▸ poor tax planning

▸ inept investing

▸ too much dependence on social security

▸ retiring too early

▸ not allowing for longer life expectancies

▸ procrastination

▸ inflation

Each of these can impede your comfortable retirement, but they don't have to. Through awareness and effort, many of the problems people face in accumulating resources for retirement can be overcome.

The Effects of Inflation on Retirement

Inflation makes it difficult to plan for retirement because you are aiming at a moving target. Your planning is made even more challenging because the effects of inflation are hard to predict. That makes it nearly impossible to predict how much money you'll need to live during your retirement years. Compared to the early 1980s, the inflation rate in the late 1990s is rather moderate. However, even with a four percent annual inflation rate, something that costs $1,000 today will cost $1,480 in 10 years. The cost will double in approximately 10 years if the inflation rate increases to seven percent. Could anyone comprehend back in the 1960s that today we would be paying $15 for a haircut, $7 for a movie, or $1 for a soft drink from a vending machine? The following table illustrates the increase in cost of a few select items.

Average Price	1970	1980	1997
postage stamp	.06	.15	.32
loaf of bread	.23	.43	$1.40
automobile	$3,400	$6,900	$18,000
house	$25,600	$64,000	$108,000

You can't think of today's dollar values when you think about retiring 5, 10, or 20 years from now. The following chart shows the inflation multiples needed at age 65 with various rates of inflation.

Current age/inflation rate chart

Age Today	3%	4%	5%	6%	7%
60	1.16	1.22	1.28	1.34	1.40
58	1.23	1.32	1.41	1.50	1.61
56	1.30	1.42	1.55	1.69	1.84
54	1.38	1.54	1.71	1.90	2.10
52	1.47	1.67	1.89	2.13	2.41
50	1.56	1.80	2.08	2.40	2.76
48	1.65	1.95	2.29	1.69	3.16
46	1.75	2.11	2.53	3.03	3.62
44	1.86	2.28	2.79	3.40	4.14
42	1.97	2.46	3.07	3.82	4.74
40	2.09	2.67	3.39	4.29	5.43
35	2.43	3.24	4.32	5.74	7.61

For example, if a person is 50 with an expected four percent inflation rate, she will need to multiply 1.80 times what an item costs today to determine the cost of that same item when she is

114

age 65. That can be kind of frightening. But don't panic—plan ahead so you're ready.

When and How to Prepare

Published reports regarding individual or family assets set aside for retirement are rather bleak in their financial projections. Many people have no assets or pension income. It's a troubling thought, but it appears that many of us will enter retirement unprepared. The income for most of us for retirement will come from three sources: savings, social security, and pensions. Most of us will receive *something* from social security, but not everyone will receive pension income. Many of us have either not worked with a company that offered a pension plan, or never became vested in any plan.

The lesson? Start planning and saving for retirement early because your personal savings and investments most likely represent a significant source of your retirement income. Get used to the idea that the combination of pension (if you even have one) and social security will probably fall short of your needs at retirement. The more income you've enjoyed during your working years, the more you will need to rely on your savings in retirement. There are some logical steps to follow so that you have the necessary nest egg at retirement. If you are successful with these steps you will likely be prepared for retirement:

1. Eliminate debt (credit cards first).

2. Create an emergency fund (approximately three months of expenses).

3. Contribute to retirement plans (401(k) or 403(b) plans and IRAs).

4. Eliminate mortgage interest payments.

5. Create retirement assets.

Planning for retirement should be a lifetime effort but realistically, the financial demands during early adulthood make it difficult for most of us to save for retirement. Those of us who have the opportunity for corporate 401(k) plans or nonprofit 403(b) plans should invest in them when possible. These plans are ideal for building up a retirement account because of the tax advantages. If you treat your monthly investment in these plans as a fixed expense, you will be more likely to stay with the plans.

To get yourself in a position to save and invest, you must first pay off all your existing loans. Because of high interest rates, credit card debt should be the first to go, followed by installment debt, and eventually the home mortgage. To get out of debt means that you can't live for the moment but must be willing to go without when necessary.

Planning for retirement and a commitment to saving go hand in hand. Preparing yourself for retirement requires serious dedication to saving. A retirement nest egg will not happen overnight. But, as with other things that are "good for you" such as exercise and eating right, once you get going on the process, it becomes easier. The flip side of saving is getting your spending under control—exercise doesn't do much for you if you're eating pizza and ice cream for every meal. You may find it necessary to adjust your lifestyle to spend less than you make for an extended period of time.

Like exercise, the concept is fairly simple—if you don't save, you lose the opportunity to accumulate a retirement nest egg. Let's take another look at an IRA plan. The table below shows the effects of an IRA retirement plan that begins at three different ages:

$2,000 invested per year at 8 percent until the age of 65

Beginning Age	Total Invested	Account Value at Age 65
25	$80,000	$561,562
35	$60,000	$246,692
45	$40,000	$100,846

The sooner you start saving, the sooner you start benefiting from the "miracle" of compound interest. The longer you wait to save, the less time your money has to work for you. So how do you start the process?

Paying off your home mortgage. It is the American dream to buy a home and with the realization of that dream normally comes a large mortgage. There is some wisdom in paying the mortgage off early. For every dollar borrowed on a long-term mortgage, you pay nearly $3 in interest; therefore, it makes good financial sense in most cases to pay it off quickly. For example, on a 30-year $100,000 loan at 10 percent interest, by adding $197 each month to your payment, you reduce the mortgage to 15 years and save $122,500 in interest. You would be spending $35,460 (197 × 180 months), but saving $122,500 in interest.

Paying off the home mortgage in 15 years provides some nice options after the house is clear of debt. In the above example, not having to pay the monthly mortgage of $1,075 per month provides extra money to spend, travel, or invest. If the $1,075 each month is invested at 10 percent for 10 years, it will grow to $226,153.

Before you contemplate prepaying your mortgage, find out if there is a prepayment penalty. Some mortgages have penalty clauses but will waive small prepayments. Check it out before you start prepaying.

There are other ways to increase your savings and decrease your spending. Fill out the following worksheet with ways that you will prepare for retirement.

Method	Monthly Amount
Increase income (e.g., part-time job):	
Reduce expenses (e.g., eat out less):	
Reduce credit and debt (e.g., get rid of credit cards):	
Reduce taxes (e.g., invest in 401(k) plan):	
Change investments (e.g., invest in growth mutual funds):	

Sources of Retirement Income

Let's review the main sources of retirement income: working wages, social security, pensions, and savings. How do you know how much of each you'll need? According to a survey conducted by the Social Security Administration, the average percentages are:

Income Source	Percentage
Social Security	38%
Assets	27%
Earnings	16%
Pensions	14%
Other	5%

So what do these averages mean for you? Do you have a pension or will you need to provide for that percentage some other way? How reliable is social security going to be by the time you retire? Let's look more closely at a couple of those categories.

Social Security. For as long as you work, you pay a percentage of your salary into the social security system. Your contributions and those of your employer are credited to your individual nine-digit number. Americans have paid ever increasing amounts to social security since its inception in the 1930s. In 1937, a worker had a maximum of $30 per year taken out of his

paycheck. By 1950 it was $45; 1960, $144; 1970, $374; 1980, $1,586. Those earning up to $65,400 in 1997 will pay 7.65 percent of that or $5,003. In addition, if you earn above $65,400 you continue paying the 1.45 percent Medicare tax. Even with the increased social security taxes, the benefits will not, for most of us, cover our retirement needs. In fact, in its own literature, the Social Security Administration points out that social security payments are not intended to finance total retirement but rather to supplement other sources of income.

If you are young, you should be concerned whether the social security system will be solvent when you retire. There is a great deal of financial stress on the solvency of the social security system. When it was first implemented in the 1930s, Americans lived to an average age of 63. With retirement age set at 65, the social security system didn't plan to pay a lot of benefits. Our longer life expectancies and earlier retirements have put greater financial pressures on social security than it has experienced in the past or than it was intended to withstand.

When social security began, there were approximately 14 contributors for every potential retiree. By 1990 that figure had declined to approximately four workers for every retiree; by 2010 it is estimated that we may see it decline to an approximate 3-to-1 ratio. (See the table below: More Retirees, Fewer Workers.) This reduced ratio will make it difficult to support the system. To prevent a social security failure, the government will likely have to substantially increase the social security tax, delay the retirement age again, or contribute a large sum of capital.

More Retirees, Fewer Workers		
	Social Security Recipients	Recipients per 100 Workers
1996	44 million	31
2000	46 million	32
2005	50 million	33
2010	54 million	34
2015	61 million	38
2020	68 million	42
2025	76 million	46
2030	81 million	49

Source: Social Security Administration

Before looking at what income you can expect from social security, let's look at when you can receive benefits. For people born in 1938 or before, the benefit age is still 65. For each year of birth after 1938 the retirement age is extended two months until birth years between 1943 and 1954 when the retirement age is set at 66. Beginning in the birth year of 1955 the retirement age again increases by two months per year until birth years 1960 or later, when the retirement age stays at 67. Current retirees can receive their payouts by percentage as follows:

	Age 65	Age 64	Age 63	Age 62
Worker	100%	93%	87%	80%
Worker's spouse	50%	45%	41%	37.5%

As shown above, a nonworking spouse will receive one-half the worker's benefits at normal retirement age. Some of the factors you may consider in deciding whether to take a reduced social security payout at age 62 are health, life expectancy, job satisfaction, and marital status. At the death of the working spouse the nonworking spouse will receive 100 percent of the benefits of the working spouse.

The social security benefits you receive during retirement are determined by the earned income that is taxed during your working years. If you worked at least 40 calendar quarters during your life, you receive retirement benefits. Today, the maximum monthly payout at retirement to the working spouse is about $1,200. Many insured workers will receive less than the maximum since their income was less than the maximum earned income subject to the social security tax. For husbands and wives who are both employed, their separate earnings determine the amount of income they receive.

Everyone should periodically contact the Social Security Administration for a benefit estimate, to check for mistakes on your work history. To receive an "Earnings and Benefit Estimate Statement," call 1-800-772-1213 from a touch-tone phone. You will be asked a choice of options from which you should choose option 2: Information about your earnings or future social security benefits. You will be asked to spell out your name and address and the form will be sent to you within two weeks.

Pension Plan Income. Many companies offer excellent pension plans that reward employees for their length of service. About 40 million Americans are covered by defined-benefit pension plans. Under these plans a company agrees to pay specified benefits to its retired employees. The amount of the plan distribution at retirement is normally computed using a combination of earned income, years of service, and age. For example, to compute the monthly benefits at retirement, companies will often pay 1.5 percent times the monthly earnings times the years of service. If the final years of service are used for the retirement calculation, it is to your benefit because those earnings are probably higher than your initial earnings with the company. If an employee stays with a corporation 30+ years, he could receive 30–40 percent of his preretirement income.

Other qualified pension plans are defined-contribution or profit-sharing plans and 401(k) plans. In contrast to the defined-benefit plan, the contribution plan is set up so the company invests a set dollar amount per month on behalf of its employees. What you receive at retirement is determined by the amount of money invested and the return on those investments. The 401(k) plan allows you as an employee to set aside a portion of your pretax salary for your own retirement planning. Some companies will also contribute to a 401(k) plan by matching a part of the employee's contribution. If you are fortunate to have a generous pension plan coupled with social security, you have covered a good portion of your financial needs at retirement.

Savings Needed at Retirement

It is a general rule of thumb that you will need between 70 and 80 percent of your present income when you retire. If this is true, pension money and social security will fall short of your goal. You will need additional sources of income, most likely from savings. The question is how much savings do you need? As mentioned earlier, inflation makes planning difficult because inflation can erode the purchasing power of a fixed retirement income. The following calculations will help you determine how much you need to save.

Determining Savings and Income Needs for Retirement

The following steps are used to determine the amount of money needed to save and invest each year to keep existing principal intact. The retiree(s) would live off the interest.

1. Your income needs at retirement will likely be less than when you worked.

    Estimated Income = 75% of preretirement income
    .75 × $_____ = $_____
           Current Income   Projected Income Needs

Projected Income needs adjusted for inflation.

$$\$\underline{\hspace{3cm}} \times \underline{\hspace{3cm}} = \underline{\hspace{3cm}}$$

Projected Income Needs   Inflation Factor   **Inflation Projected Income Needs**

(See table 1 for inflation factor.)

Table 1

Years to retirement	5	10	15	20	25	30
Inflation factor 4%	1.22	1.48	1.80	2.19	2.67	3.24
5%	1.28	1.63	2.08	2.65	3.39	4.32
6%	1.34	1.79	2.40	3.21	4.29	5.74
8%	1.47	2.16	3.17	4.66	6.85	10.06

2. Sources of income during retirement

   Current estimated annual benefits

   Social Security $\$\underline{\hspace{4cm}}$

   Pension $\$\underline{\hspace{4cm}}$

   Inflation adjusted annual benefits at retirement (using table 1)

   Social Security $\$\underline{\hspace{4cm}}$

   Pension $\$\underline{\hspace{4cm}}$

   Total $\$\underline{\hspace{4cm}}$

3. Determining shortfall (if any)

$$\$\underline{\hspace{3cm}} - \$\underline{\hspace{3cm}} = \underline{\hspace{3cm}}$$

Inflation Projected   Inflation Adjusted   Projected Annual
Income Need   S.S. and Pension   Income Shortfall
(From step 1 above)   (From step 2 above)   (Inflation adjusted)

4. Needed savings, if any, to offset annual income shortfall.

$$\$\underline{\hspace{3cm}} \div \underline{\hspace{3cm}} = \$\underline{\hspace{2cm}}$$

Projected Annual   Future Investment Return   Savings needed
Income Shortfall   4%, 5%, 6%, etc.   at retirement
(Inflation adjusted)   (.04, .05, .06, etc.)   (Inflation adjusted)

5. To find the current value of the needed savings, use the present value factor in the table:

Table 2

Years to Retirement	5	10	15	20	25	30
Present Value with projected investment results 4%	.822	.676	.555	.456	.375	.308
5%	.784	.614	.481	.377	.295	.231
6%	.747	.558	.417	.312	.233	.174
8%	.681	.463	.315	.215	.146	.099

_____ × \$_____ = _____
Present value factor   Savings needed at   Current savings
(from table 2)   retirement   needed
     (Inflation adjusted)
     (from step 4)

_____ – \$_____ = _____
Current savings needed   Existing savings   Current savings (shortfall or excess)

6. Find the projected growth of existing savings with an estimated investment return. (See table 1 for investment growth factors of 4%, 5%, 6%, or 8%.)

\$_____ × _____ = \$_____
Existing savings   Growth factor   Projected growth of
     existing savings

\$_____ – \$_____ = \$_____
Savings needed at   Projected growth of   Future savings needed
retirement   existing savings
(from step 4)

7. To determine how much you need to invest per year until retirement with an estimated investment return, use the future sum of an annuity table.

Growth Annuity Table

Years to Retirement	5	10	15	20	25	30
Growth annuity 4%	5.416	12.006	20.024	29.778	41.646	56.085
5%	5.526	12.578	21.579	33.066	47.427	66.434
6%	5.637	13.181	23.276	36.786	54.865	79.058
8%	5.867	14.987	27.152	45.762	73.106	113.28

$\$$_____ – _____ = $\$$_____

Future savings needed (from step 6)	Factor from growth annuity table	Amount needed to invest per year

Through this exercise, you have just calculated the recommended amount that should be invested yearly in order to have adequate funds for retirement.

IRA Roll Over

If you retire with a pension plan, or in some cases, reach the age of 70 ½, you will be faced with several options. Possible alternatives could include taking a lump sum distribution from your pension plan and paying the income tax, accepting an annuity over your lifetime, or rolling the plan into an IRA.

The least attractive option from an income tax perspective is taking a lump sum distribution and paying the income tax. If you roll over your pension into an IRA, the full amount is available for investment, and you maximize the potential balance available for retirement purposes. This roll-over process avoids current income taxation of your pension plan assets. To avoid a 20 percent withholding tax upon transfer, ensure that your pension plan balance is paid directly to the IRA custodian.

The following distribution rules should help you understand how to handle your IRA and other retirement plans responsibly.

Prior to age 59 ½: If you withdraw assets prior to age 59 ½, you incur a 10 percent penalty tax. This tax is in addition to the income tax that will be due.

After age 70 ½: Beginning at age 70 ½, partial distributions are mandatory. If the distribution is less than what is necessary, there is a 50 percent penalty on the amount of distribution not made.

Insurance Issues

While life insurance continues to offer needed protection during retirement, health insurance becomes an issue of paramount importance. The goal should be to protect yourself, your family, and your retirement funds as simply and as cost effectively as possible. Disability insurance may be important if you need to work during retirement, but it may no longer be necessary to continue paying the premium. Check with your insurance provider.

Health Insurance. Most retirees live on fixed incomes so lack of good medical coverage could be disastrous. A serious health problem without insurance could eliminate all retirement savings; you may have an employer-sponsored health plan but if you don't you will need individual health policies. Shop around for the best coverage at the best price. If you are healthy, consider high deductible policies so you can save on your premiums.

Joining a health maintenance organization (HMO) can often be a money-saving way to acquire complete health coverage. For a set monthly fee, you can obtain a family plan and pay as little as $10 per doctor visit, although you may have to give up your current doctors if they are not affiliated with that particular plan.

After age 65, you are eligible for Medicare, which is offered through the U.S. Department of Health and Human Services. Medicare pays only part of your health expenses. You need to supplement the coverage. With Part A (or Medicare hospital insurance) you are automatically covered if you are entitled to social security benefits. Part B, or Medicare's Medical Insurance program, is an optional program that requires you to pay monthly premiums.

Life Insurance. Can your family carry on financially without you? If the answer is no, examine your current life insurance and decide if you need more. If you already own whole-life insurance, you may be covered adequately. For additional insurance, consider term insurance, which provides the most coverage for the lowest cost.

When looking for life insurance, pay attention to the ratings of the insurer. A.M. Best Co. evaluates insurance carriers. It is advisable to buy insurance from those companies that receive an A++, A+, or A in A.M. Best's evaluation. To find the ratings, consult *Best's Agents Guide* or *Best's Insurance Reports* in the library. For further information on the ratings of insurance companies, call 1-900-555-2378.

Long-term Care. Long-term care insurance, virtually unknown a decade ago, is growing faster than most other forms of insurance. Long-term care is day-in, day-out assistance you may need if you can't care for yourself. Financially speaking, long-term care is one of the greatest financial challenges facing senior citizens. Some people will attempt to insure themselves, which means their retirement nest eggs will need to cover $30,000 to $50,000 per year. Nursing home care is very expensive and costs are rising. For many whose nest eggs are insufficient to cover these costs, long-term care insurance has come to the rescue. The premiums you pay for long-term care insurance will depend on your age, health, and the choices you make, but the annual premiums can be in the thousands. If you

124

choose to buy long-term care insurance, your policies should contain the following:

1. A prior stay in the hospital should not be required.

2. The policy should be adjusted to inflation.

3. The policy should be guaranteed renewable for life.

4. Home care should be included.

5. The policy should allow for a waiver of premium if its owner is institutionalized.

Insurance premiums will be much cheaper if you begin paying the premium in your 40s or 50s. Remember, it's buyer beware. It is to your advantage to compare several policies before you make your final choice.

Unfortunately, the nation's largest health-care program, Medicare, covers only a fraction of nursing home expenses. Its companion, Medicaid, pays the nursing home bill, but only for those who are without funds. To qualify, you must first spend most of your assets.

A study by the U.S. Department of Health and Human Services indicates that 65-year-old persons face at least a 40 percent chance of entering a nursing home and about 10 percent will stay there for five years or longer. Because women generally outlive men by several years, they face a 50 percent greater likelihood than men of entering a nursing home after age 65. The study also shows how long nursing home care normally lasts:

Length of Stay	% of Patients
0–30 days	31
1–3 months	21
3–6 months	11
6–9 months	7
9–12 months	5
12–24 months	10
24–36 months	5
over 36 months	11
(Total rounds off to equal 101 percent.)	

According to this study, 75 percent of the people going to a nursing home will be there for 12 months or less. This information may be helpful in deciding your long-term care insurance needs.

Insurance premiums probably aren't your favorite expense, but your financial health is at risk if you don't have health, life, disability, and possibly long-term care insurance. Insurance can be a blessing when it provides for the needs of surviving family members after a death, pays for major surgery, or supports the long-term care for a senior citizen. Be responsible and buy insurance when the potential for financial loss is high but be prudent and shop around to acquire the best coverage at a reasonable price.

Retirement Savings Needed by Women

According to *USA Today* (May 29, 1996), women tend to save less money for retirement than men. Women generally have less disposable cash to set aside and their investments tend to be too conservative, preventing good growth of their savings. However, women, on average, tend to live longer than men, so they should have larger savings. Women also need larger retirement savings because of their work patterns. According to the Labor Department, the median pension for women is half that for men and two out of three women are in jobs that don't provide retirement benefits. Women face many disadvantages in preparing for retirement, including the following:

▸ Because of family responsibilities, women tend to spend fewer years working.

▸ Women, on average, earn approximately three-fourths of what men earn and change jobs more frequently. The smaller income and greater job turnover cause reduced retirement benefits.

▸ Women are more likely than men to work part-time.[22]

The trend may be changing, but currently many women face a greater retirement challenge than men. Women especially need to carefully evaluate their retirement benefits, make a greater effort to save more, and be more aggressive on investments. Know how the laws and trends affect you and plan for your future—fair or not.

Forced Retirement

Corporate restructuring has forced hundreds of thousands of individuals into early retirement. Unplanned retirement often creates a financial crisis if you are not ready for it. If you find yourself out of work at an older age, you are likely going to find it more difficult to get back to work—especially the work you want to do. If you are forced to retire a few years early, you may have to rethink your retirement plans because the money won't be there.

If you lose your job, you may need to overcome depression before you can meet the challenge head-on. Update your résumé and move forward. First, contact as many individuals and companies as possible. Especially if you are of retirement age, the phone probably won't be ringing; you will need to initiate the calls. You may want to consult a book on midlife career changes or talk to a career counselor.

Looking forward to those golden years in retirement? Will they be filled with travel opportunities, sipping iced tea on the patio or at the lakeshore, playing golf, or serving in the church? For many, the retirement lifestyle they anticipated and hoped for will not be a reality.

Whether due to procrastination, unwillingness to sacrifice current pleasures, lack of saving, no planning, or poor investing, many of us will not have the resources to provide the retirement lifestyle we want. And inflation continues to rise. And people are living longer. Is there any hope? Yes, but it requires a process of planning and developing strategies for providing for a comfortable retirement. Only you know what you want your retirement years to be like and only you can plan ahead to achieve them.

Questions for Personal Reflection

Use the following questions to help you focus on your understanding of retirement.

1. Jesus came to redeem us and to _____ (Matthew 20:28).

2. What do we gain in serving (1 Timothy 3:13)?

3. How are we to serve God (Deuteronomy 10:12; Joshua 22:5)?

4. We are to serve the Lord and who else (Galatians 5:13–14)?

6. What does Titus 2:14 say about the interest we should have to do good deeds?

7. As God's stewards, we are blessed with the "fruit of the Spirit" found in Galatians 5:22–23. Because the "fruit of the Spirit" often develops in a lifelong maturing process, can more be expected of individuals in retirement years?

8. Are our churches getting our senior citizens involved? Are we tapping into their experience and gifts? In your church, are retired individuals serving in leadership positions?

9. Why would eliminating credit card and installment debt be an important first step rather than putting money in savings?

Chapter 8

Making a Planned Gift

Many of us will have the privilege of giving gifts of stocks, real estate, or savings during our lifetimes or when we die. With proper planning, gifting can give support to as well as provide tax reduction and other economic benefits for Christian causes and other charities.

One man gives freely, yet gains even more; another withholds unduly, but comes to poverty.
Proverbs 11:24

We can look at giving as an outward expression of our spiritual values and our love for God. In this chapter we will focus on opportunities we have to give gifts of real estate, securities, insurance policies, personal property, collectibles, and other savings.

As God's people, we have been materially blessed in different proportions. Some of us have an abundance while others have very little. What matters is what we do with what we are given because we are all called to be faithful and diligent managers of God's property. If God in His wisdom has blessed us with material wealth, we have an added responsibility. Those with extra money can help those who are without. "At the present time your plenty will supply what they need, so that in turn their plenty will supply what you need. Then there will be equality" (2 Corinthians 8:14). We are blessed to be a blessing to others.

Every generation makes an impression on humanity. Much of what this country has accomplished is due to the generosity of those who proceeded us. Many institutions, colleges, and other nonprofit organizations that serve us have been and are being supported by generous and giving people. Charity is one the cornerstones of this nation.

As a nation, we recognize the importance of charitable giving and encourage it. Our country has tax laws that offer special income, gift, and estate tax advantages for those who contribute to qualified charities. Our government, through its tax laws, is encouraging us to give through well-established gifting techniques. The tax laws promote and help develop a potentially better future.

Planned Giving

It is exciting to be able to make a financial contribution to help spread the Gospel. A planned gift can also help you do some financial planning to prepare for the future. A planned gift is an opportunity to give the biggest gift of your life. A professionally trained counselor representing churches or other charities can talk to you about tax implications and various ways to give. A planned gift can be defined as follows:

1. A gift of any kind for any amount given for any purpose, whether for current operations, capital expansion, or endowment. It may be given either now as a current gift or later as a deferred gift. The gift is often done with a professionally trained counselor.

2. A planned gift is usually driven or motivated by the donor's needs, not the nonprofit institution's needs.

3. A planned gift offers older donors ways to give while maintaining financial security and economic freedom.

4. Planned giving often makes charitable giving affordable, and it enables the donor to give larger gifts than originally thought possible.[23]

Planned Giving is a tool. Planned giving is a win-win situation. Both the giver and the recipient benefit. Planned giving can help the person giving the gift as well as the individual or institution receiving it in the following ways:

1. The charity (such as a church, seminary, college, etc.) can use the gift to conduct its ministry and reach its goals.

2. Your gift can help you fulfill your need to be a good steward. You demonstrate good stewardship when you faithfully share your resources.

3. Planned gifts can help provide income and security for others, including the disabled or elderly.

4. A planned gift can provide for family or friends through a gift in your last will and testament.

5. Your gift may provide some tax benefits for you through charitable deductions.

6. Your gifts can provide for an annual income for yourself and your family members.

7. Your gifts can benefit the Lord's work after your death.

8. Investing in a charitable gift instrument, as explained later in this chapter, can eliminate your investment management worries.

Planning the planned gift. First, assess your current financial situation. If you haven't already developed net worth statements (see chapter 2), do so. Review the goals you've developed to see if your resources will allow you to fulfill them. By reviewing all your resources, needs, and goals, you will get a good picture of what you have and what you need to accomplish your financial goals. Before considering a gift, determine the amount of income needed for living expenses, looking beyond current needs and projecting the needs for retirement. If you consider a bequest at death, can the gift be made and still maintain adequate resources to provide for family members? You may not want to consider a gift if it will cause a financial hardship for others.

The planned gift may be a gift of excess assets that you freely give, without any desire for a tax break. At other times, your desire to give may be prompted by your interest in receiving tax benefits and/or an income flow. Most planned gifts need to have some charitable intent because even the tax breaks and income together can't entirely replace the money or value of the assets given.

Personal sacrifice. Today's society is fast-paced, complex, and draining, physically and emotionally. In all your turmoil and stress, you may be looking for a greater purpose and meaning for life. As a Christian, God has been and continues to be your source of strength and reason for living. In addition to supporting your church and other Christian ministries financially, you find value and purpose when you identify, associate with, and support worthwhile programs, causes, and organizations.

Gaining wealth only for wealth's sake does not provide lasting satisfaction. When your money can be directed to support causes that promote God's kingdom, eliminate suffering, provide social equality, and improve the environment, you receive meaning in life and personal satisfaction. It is meaningful to give money, but money is a poor substitute for not giving of ourselves. The most valuable gift we can give is a portion of ourselves. Thank God daily that you are enabled by the Holy Spirit to be generous. It is God who gives through us, and it is He who is to receive the praise and glory. "You will be made rich in every way so that you can be generous on every occasion, and through us your generosity will result in thanksgiving to God" (2 Corinthians 9:11).

What to give. For many of us, our only giving experience is with cash, but other assets that we own may be more appropriate to give. If you give appreciated stocks, mutual funds, or real estate to charity, you not only receive a charitable income tax deduction, but you eliminate the capital gains tax. The effective cost of giving is made easier and less expensive, bypassing any capital gains taxes and reducing income and estate taxes when necessary. If you have assets that have dropped in value from the original purchase price, it is to your advantage to sell those investments for tax losses and then give the proceeds to the charity. By selling before you give, you are entitled to take the income tax deduction created by your loss of principal on your personal tax return. Nonprofit organizations do not receive any tax loss benefits.

You may want to consider giving whole-life insurance policies. Often, family circumstances change so that insurance policies are no longer needed. For example, when your children are young, you likely need a larger amount of insurance protection. However, when the children are grown, you may have less need for insurance coverage. If you give an insurance policy, the insurance company will calculate the income tax deduction you will receive.

Our giving could include antiques, paintings, farm equipment, collectibles, etc. For tax purposes, understand that personal property often does not allow for the full fair market value deduction. These items are likely to receive a deduction for the original purchase price (the cost basis) of the item given.

You can make a planned gift in your last will and testament. Your will or trust can be a final testimony of your love and faith in Jesus Christ, and you can put that love into action through a bequest. The assets you accumulate during your lifetime can possibly provide the best opportunity for you to make a major gift. Paul says in 1 Timothy 6:17–19:

> Command those who are rich in this present world not to be arrogant nor to put their hope in wealth, which is so uncertain, but to put their hope in God, who richly provides us with everything for our enjoyment. Command them to do good, to be rich in good deeds, and to be generous and willing to share. In this way they will lay up treasure for themselves as a firm foundation for the coming age, so that they may take hold of the life that is truly life.

If gifts will be made at the time of death, the best choice of assets to give will be different than during your lifetime. At death, appreciated property is not subject to capital gains so those assets do not offer any tax incentives for gifting. Retirement benefit plans such as 401(k)s, 403(b)s, and IRAs have the largest transfer tax consequences at death. The income taxes that you've been able to defer during your lifetime are due when retirement plans are terminated by death. The only exception to this is when, at death, the principal from the plans is given directly to charity or placed into a Charitable Remainder Trust (CRT). The money placed into a CRT offered by a charity can avoid the income tax liability. An individual may have his retirement plan beneficiary form designate part or all the funds to go into the CRT. The Charitable Remainder Trust will provide income for the surviving family members for life or up to 20 years. When the CRT is dissolved, the principal remaining in the CRT is given to the charity the donor has chosen.

The following diagram shows the tax consequences of retirement benefit plans at death.

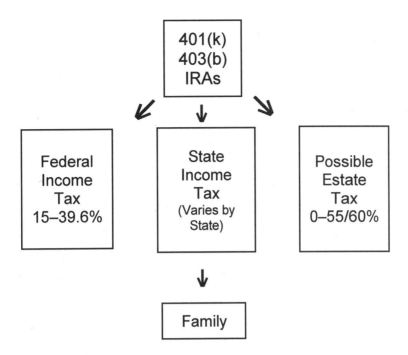

```
          ┌──────────┐
          │  401(k)  │
          │  403(b)  │
          │   IRAs   │
          └──────────┘
        ↙       ↓       ↘
┌──────────┐ ┌──────────┐ ┌──────────┐
│ Federal  │ │  State   │ │ Possible │
│ Income   │ │  Income  │ │  Estate  │
│   Tax    │ │   Tax    │ │   Tax    │
│ 15–39.6% │ │(Varies by│ │ 0–55/60% │
│          │ │  State)  │ │          │
└──────────┘ └──────────┘ └──────────┘
                  ↓
            ┌──────────┐
            │  Family  │
            └──────────┘
```

Without proper planning the money remaining in retirement plans can be heavily taxed.

There is a story about a wealthy man in a small town who passed away. After his death, the townspeople were betting as to how much he left behind. Each guess was wrong—he left it all behind.

You can take nothing with you but, if you make certain your money will work for you after your death, in the truest sense, you have taken it with you. If the needs of your family have been met and you give money or possessions to the Lord's work, you have left a living memorial. Your life work, after death, goes on benefiting God's kingdom.

Voluntary versus involuntary giving. At your death the assets you have accumulated during your life will ultimately go to your family, the government, or charity. Through proper planning, you can determine which of the three entities receives a greater share of your estate.

If you don't make any plans, the IRS will maximize what it can take from your estate and the government will decide how it spends your money. Through voluntary giving or philanthropy, you determine what church, charity, or cause you want your estate to benefit. Your giving can also lessen your estate tax liabilities, if any, which reduces the net cost of your generosity. Reducing your taxes allows you to have more for your family and your favorite ministries or charities.

Following are examples of wealthy individuals who did no estate or tax planning and examples of some who did plan. Most people's estates aren't this large, but the same principles apply.

Name	Gross Estate	% Lost to Taxes
Those who did not plan:		
Charles Woolworth, *F. W. Woolworth Co.*	$16,788,702	62%
Elvis Presley, *Entertainer*	$10,165,434	72%
Jessica Savitch, *NBC News Anchor*	$2,175,463	51%
Those who did plan:		
John Rockefeller, Sr., *Founder, Standard Oil*	$17,124,988	3%
William R. Hearst, *Publisher*	$57,115,167	6%
Waite Phillips, *Oilman*	$10,246,258	6%[24]

Those individuals who did tax planning decided they were more interested in a charity than the government receiving the assets they had worked hard to accumulate. By not creating a charitable giving plan, the other individuals allowed more than half of their estates to be lost in taxes.

Planned Giving Motivation

In addition to our love, faith, and obedience to Christ, we can experience other motivations to give:

▸ *Sense of Philanthropy.* If we give because we wish to improve the world and have a sense of duty, we are philanthropists.

▸ *Gratitude.* We may have been blessed by an organization to which we would like to show our appreciation. Churches and educational or social institutions will receive our thank offerings.

▸ *Guilt Obligation.* A guilty conscience is certainly a motivator that causes us to feel we must give.

▸ *Tax Considerations.* Normally tax incentives will not be the only reason to give, but they may initiate or enhance the size of the gift. We can benefit from avoiding capital gains tax and eliminating or reducing federal, estate, and income taxes.

▸ *Belief in Missions.* We often find causes that speak to our hearts, which will prompt financial support.

▸ *Community Responsibility and Civic Pride.* Many of us will want to perpetuate, through our giving, neighborhoods and communities where we have lived.

▸ *Honoring Loved Ones.* Gifts are made as memorial tributes to honor loved ones.

▸ *Recognition.* We often like to be recognized and to receive attention for our giving.

▸ *Financial Benefit.* Nonprofit organizations often provide gift instruments that can provide an investor with an income return.

▸ *Appeal of Promotional Pieces.* We may get excited over a letter or brochure we receive and it causes us to give.

▸ *Social Standing and Prestige.* A contribution may be the ticket or opportunity to become one of the insiders of an organization.

▸ *Potential of Living Longer.* Studies suggest that giving creates an improved emotional and physical state, causing a longer life.

▸ *Regard for Staff Leadership.* We often will give to an organization because of the people who represent that institution.

Thank God daily that there are so many committed people who want to make a difference in this world. Life takes on a new perspective when we believe we can, in a small way, improve life for others.

Categories of Giving

Outright. Cash is the most common outright gift. An outright gift has no strings attached. Giving cash is convenient and straightforward. For income tax purposes, you receive a 100 percent deduction for your cash gift. The only exception is if your cash gifts exceed, in any one year, 50 percent of your adjusted gross income (AGI). Gifts that exceed 50 percent of your AGI can be deducted over the next five years. You can classify property for charitable giving by the following criteria:

1. cash

2. ordinary income property (life insurance)

3. long-term capital gain property (stocks, real estate)

4. tangible personal property (art, equipment)

An added advantage for gifting any appreciated assets would be saving capital gain taxes. If you give appreciated property, the tax laws only allow a maximum deduction of 30 percent of your adjusted gross income versus 50 percent for cash.

Split-interest Gift. A split-interest gift may be given both during your life and/or at your death. In contrast to an outright gift, there are strings attached to a split-interest. With a split-interest gift you keep some benefits (such as income for a period of time). For this type of gift, there is a partial deduction for the value of the assets given. Split-interest gifts can be illustrated as follows:

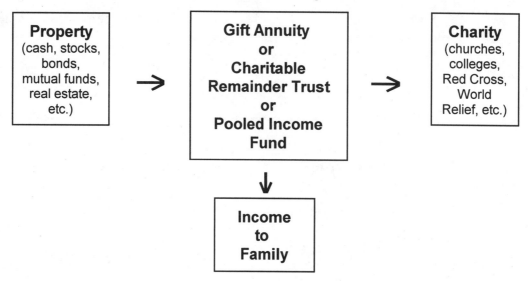

Split-interest gifts include:

A. Gift Annuities

A gift annuity is an excellent way to use your material blessings to provide for both your family and for the Lord's work. This method provides:

- ◆ regular fixed payments for life;

- ◆ significant tax savings (partial income tax deductions, partial tax free payments, and possible estate tax reductions);

- ◆ a way to make a future gift to spread the Gospel.

Many nonprofit organizations make Gift Annuities available as an investment. Investors can invest, for most charities, a minimum of $1,000 in cash or securities. The investors will receive from their Gift Annuities income distributions that will be paid to them throughout their lives. The Gift Annuity can be set up with a second individual, who will continue to receive the income after the death of the first. In addition to the income, investors also receive the joy of knowing that their investments will benefit the charities of their choices following their deaths.

Many people like Gift Annuities because the size of the distribution check remains constant. The annual income is determined by the age of the income recipient. At the death of one or both donors, the charity receives the remaining value. The Gift Annuity is irrevocable, which means once the investment is made no changes can be made.

Gift Annuity rates suggested by the Committee on Gift Annuities as of March 1997 are:

Age	Rate
30	6.0%
40	6.2%
50	6.5%
60	6.9%
70	7.7%
80	9.4%
90+	12.0%

The committee normally sets new rates every three to four years. For example, a 60-year-old person who invested $1,000 would annually receive $69.

B. Charitable Remainder Trust

To establish a Charitable Remainder Trust (CRT) you irrevocably place cash, securities, real estate or other property into a trust from which you receive income for life or a specified period of time. After you transfer the property, the charity or trustee for the charity determines whether to keep your transferred assets as an investment of the CRT or to sell them. If the trustee feels that the best course of action is to sell the asset, then the trustee determines how to reinvest the proceeds. There are many reasons that a CRT may be advantageous:

▸ Desire to make a major gift for the Lord's work.

▸ The need for a lifetime income for yourself and your spouse as well as an additional 20 years for the children (normally paid quarterly).

▸ Avoiding capital gains tax.

▸ To improve current income.

▸ Desire to reduce or eliminate estate taxes and probate costs.

▸ Interest in eliminating management responsibility.

Because a CRT can't be changed once it is set up, much thought and prayer should take place before the gift is made. Many charities require a $20,000 minimum in cash and possibly a greater amount if real estate is involved. Unlike Gift Annuities, the quarterly income return from a CRT may change.

C. Pooled Income Fund

A Pooled Income Fund is a pool of gifts (investments) invested under professional management. Everyone who invests in the pool shares in the proportionate amount of income. The major difference between Pooled Income Funds and Gift Annuities is that the income flow will vary with Pooled Funds. The distributed income is determined by the investment results.

A partial tax deduction is available in the year the investment is made. After the lifetime of the income recipient(s), the current market value of the pooled income is available for the charity. The minimum investment for most charities is approximately $1,000. The capital gains tax can be avoided when appreciated securities are invested in a Pooled Income Fund. As with Gift Annuities and Charitable Remainder Trusts, the Pooled Income Fund is irrevocable.

D. Charitable Lead Trust

A Charitable Lead Trust is the mirror image of a Charitable Remainder Trust because the charity receives income rather than the remaining principal. To set up a Charitable Lead Trust you irrevocably transfer assets to a trustee and provide that income to be paid to one or more charities for a predetermined period of time, after which the principal is either returned to you or distributed to others.

This type of gift is appropriate for individuals who have excess savings or investments and don't need any more current income. If estate taxes are a concern, a Charitable Lead Trust would be beneficial because donors can receive substantial estate tax deductions.

E. Retained Life Estate

Your biggest asset is likely to be your home. If you have an interest in giving the home you can transfer the deed to a charity while you are alive, but keep living in the house. The benefit of giving now versus later is the income tax deduction. The other benefit is experiencing the joy of giving. In a retained life estate, you would still be responsible for the cost of insurance, taxes, and upkeep.

Testamentary

A. Bequest

You have the opportunity to contribute to the Lord's work by leaving part of your accumulated assets after you die. The only way a bequest will be made is if you have a will or trust. If no will exists, your state will not give on your behalf, regardless of how active you were in the church.

The recommended giving method is through a percentage of the estate versus a specific dollar amount. With a percentage, your estate value can fluctuate and you won't need to be nervous if your estate is incapable of giving the specified amount in the will. You may want to stipulate that a bequest will only occur if your spouse is deceased or your children are no longer minors.

B. Contracts

After your death, many of your assets such as life insurance and individual retirements plans, will be passed on by contract through beneficiary form designations. In your giving through these assets, you may be interested in giving a part of your account value or 100 percent of it. The process can be accomplished by simply naming churches or other charities as beneficiaries. After your death the beneficiary forms will determine the distribution of the principal.

Making the Most Appropriate Gift

After considering all the characteristics of the various ways of giving and the tax implications of each, you can select the best way and the most appropriate assets to give. What you need and want to accomplish (in addition to your generosity) with your giving will help determine the timing, amount, and what assets you want to give. When giving is prompted by your love for Christ, for others, for a ministry, or for a cause, the tax savings and other benefits are secondary. However, when you understand the advantages of making certain types of gifts, you may be able to give more than you ever thought was possible. If you understand the advantages and disadvantages of making certain types of gifts, you can become a more effective steward. To make the most of your giving, remember the potential problems resulting from giving too soon, giving too late, giving too little, and giving too much.

Questions for Personal Reflection

Use the following questions to help you focus on your understanding of planned gifts.

1. What does Luke 12:48 say to everyone who has been given much?

2. What are the wealthy to do with their surplus (2 Corinthians 8:14)?

3. What do Jesus' words in Acts 20:35 say about giving?

4. What does sacrificial giving mean to you?

5. What promise do we find in 2 Corinthians 9:11?

6. What encouragement to give is Paul sharing in 2 Corinthians 8:1–7?

7. How was the widow of Zarephath blessed with her sacrificial giving in 1 Kings 17:7–24?

8. What does Paul say we should do with our treasures in 2 Corinthians 9:6–12?

9. What happens to all our possessions at death (1 Timothy 6:7)?

A Christian estate plan allows you a final opportunity to share your faith and to distribute your assets to both your family and the Lord's work.

A good man leaves an inheritance for his children's children, but a sinner's wealth is stored up for the righteous.
Proverbs 13:22

Why do we do estate planning? A thorough and complete estate plan is good stewardship because it reduces the expenses and taxes associated with death so that more will be available for your family and the Lord's work.

The last will and testament will be your final words to the world and to your surviving family members. You can easily get caught up in the idea that a will only deals with property, but it really deals with people. Your loved ones are the most important reasons for having a will. This formal and legal document also can be used to express how much the Lord has meant to you and to thank Him for His gifts during your lifetime. If your will contains a statement of faith that proclaims Christ and encourages your loved ones to put their faith in Him, it will be a comforting message for your family and friends to hear during their time of sorrow.

Estate planning takes time. It involves money, belongings, spouses, children, grandchildren, close friends, favorite family members, and charities. It also involves taxes, insurance policies, lawyers, banks, accountants, and financial planners. But an estate plan will express the goals that you hope to pass on to those who follow you, so it is an important tool.

The will or trust is the cornerstone of an estate plan, but other documents and planning steps are necessary as well. To accomplish an estate disposition in an effective and economical manner, reduce any possible federal estate tax obligations and the likely probate costs. In addition, consider preparing for the time when, because of health reasons, you may not be able to handle your legal and financial affairs. Examine how your assets are titled, review insurance policies, and analyze retirement assets. It's also a good idea to resolve such issues as life support continuation while you're healthy. These, as well as other topics, will be discussed in this chapter.

You Can't Take It With You

With the unpredictability of life, we realize God's timetable is not the same as ours. If the Lord took you home today, would everything be in order? Are both your spiritual and fiscal lives in good shape? Your possessions, regardless of size, will be distributed according to your wishes only if you have an updated will. A properly drafted will provides, if need be, for guardians of minor children, handicapped family members, grandchildren, friends, children, the church, and others. As important as wills are, it is estimated that nearly seven out of ten Americans die without one. It can be unpleasant to think about and plan for your own death. Many of us can find lots of other things we'd rather do. But if you've ever had to deal with the mess left by a family member or close friend who died without a will, you know how important the planning process is. Keep in mind that talking about death will not make it happen sooner and not talking about death won't delay it. Take the time and effort now to save your family the strain of dealing with your assets (and all the estate taxes) during an already emotional time.

Reasons for Not Getting the Will Done

People give many reasons for postponing or not writing a will. Do any of these sound familiar?

I don't care. The attitude "I don't care what happens to me after I'm gone" expresses the feeling "I'll be gone, so who cares?" God certainly cares. Your family cares. Who wouldn't want to take care of loved ones and plan for the proper distribution of assets? Providing for your family is a real opportunity to express your love.

I'm young. A common reason people put off completing a will is that "I'm young, and I have plenty of time." You may think you have plenty of time, but your time is in God's hands. Car accidents don't differentiate. Cancer occurs in both young and old. There is no better time than today to write your will.

Everything is in joint tenancy. If you have everything in joint tenancy with your spouse, at your death, everything outside of probate will go automatically to your surviving spouse. The surviving spouse will own it all. Joint tenancy does provide a nice estate transfer procedure, but it certainly isn't the ultimate solution. Think ahead to the death of the surviving spouse or to the possibility of a common disaster in which both lives are simultaneously lost. Also, joint tenancy ownership can potentially result in higher estate taxes because you lose the benefit of the unified credit at the death

of the first spouse (explained later under Federal Estate Tax).

I can't afford to write a will. It would be proper to turn that around and say you can't afford *not* to write a will. The added time and cost to settle an estate without a will is much greater. And there are attorneys who will write wills at a reasonable cost—perhaps there is an attorney in your congregation who gives a discount to church members. While an attorney is recommended, there are also will kits available. If you use a will kit, it's advisable to have an attorney review your will.

Procrastination. Procrastination is possibly the number one reason people give for not writing a will. If that's your excuse, find some time to get your plans in order. Promise yourself that you will have a will completed before the end of the year. Then work to make that happen. You don't have to do all your estate planning at once—take it one step at a time.

Purposes of Estate Planning

Estate planning is the creation and development of a master plan to handle the disposition of your belongings at death as well as during your lifetime. Estate planning is also an act of stewardship. For many people, the word *estate* means lots of money, stocks, or real estate. If you have that understanding, you could mistakenly assume that if you don't have much, an estate plan is unnecessary. But if you have *any* assets to leave, you need to have a plan for their distribution. Estate plans are necessary for a number of reasons:

1. An estate plan will convey your love for the Lord and your family.

2. An estate plan will ensure that your assets are distributed the way you want them to be.

3. An estate plan will minimize the time it takes for the disposition of assets.

4. An estate plan will keep estate taxes to a minimum.

5. An estate plan will keep probate and other administration costs to a minimum.

6. An estate plan will provide for the availability of accessible funds to pay any estate tax obligations.

7. An estate plan will provide for the continuation of the Lord's work.

Estate planning takes into consideration administrative and other expenses associated with death. Currently the highest progressive tax rate is the federal estate tax which is as high as 55 percent. In addition to the possible large estate and inheritance taxes, typical expenses include:

- ▸ funeral expenses
- ▸ executor's fees
- ▸ probate court fees
- ▸ legal fees

143

- ► accounting fees
- ► medical expenses
- ► appraisal fees

There is a story of a young boy who went to a pet store with his father to buy a puppy. One of the puppies was wagging his tail furiously. The dad asked the son, "Which puppy do you want?" The son, pointing to the one with the wagging tail, said, "The one with the happy ending." A completed estate plan that has properly minimized expenses and taxes, provided for loved ones, and continued your stewardship responsibly, will give your final planning a "happy ending."

What Is a Will?

A will is a legal document that sets forth how an individual's property will be disposed of at his or her death. The will leaves the property to specifically named individuals known as beneficiaries. The property transferred according to the terms of the will is known as a bequest. In most states the signing of the will has to be properly witnessed by two (or three) competent witnesses and possibly notarized. The maker of the will must be of sound mind and of legal age.

Not all states require written wills. However, the risk of a verbal will being declared invalid is high. Even do-it-yourselfers should consider leaving the drafting of wills to professionals. Wills are too important and too technical to leave to an amateur's effort. A will is one of the most important documents you will ever put together.

Wills are public documents. At the death of the maker of the will, the will is filed with the county probate court, and it can be viewed by the public. After the death of a neighbor, you could go to the court house to see his will. You could see how anyone's assets and debts were discharged.

Many believe that because a will determines the transfer of estates, it will avoid the probate process. But probate is merely the period of time where the deceased person's estate is administered under the supervision of the probate court. A will does not avoid the probate process. During probate the will is "proved" and claims against the estate are heard. Without a will, the legislature of the state of residence of the deceased determines distribution.

When writing your will, be mindful of the type of property you own and how that property is titled. Wills do not transfer property that goes by other planning devices or by operation of law. Remember joint tenancy which automatically provides that the surviving tenant becomes the legal owner of the asset regardless of what a will says? Likewise, life insurance proceeds, retirement plans, and annuities are transferred outside of a will by beneficiary forms. Your will may or may not be controlling a large portion of your estate. It's important to know what assets are and are not affected by your will.

Prior to your death, your will is revocable—it can be amended, altered, or revoked a number of times. Many wills are revised by the use of codicils, which are normally short amendments making simple changes. Changes are often made at the birth or death of immediate family members, at a

144

change in marital status, or when major property (such as a house) is bought or sold. At death the will becomes irrevocable.

What happens if I die without a will?

If you fail to make a will, the consequences include:

- Your property will be distributed according to the laws of your state.
- Your estate will be managed by court-appointed administrators—possibly people you would not choose.
- People most dear to you may not benefit.
- No gift will be made to support the work of the Lord.
- Your heirs may experience a maze of legalities that a will could have avoided.
- The laws of your state may not permit your spouse to inherit the whole estate, but divide it equally among your children and spouse.
- Administrative costs and taxes for distribution of your estates may be greater.
- You may be unable to ensure the continued operation of a family farm or business.

If you die without a will, your estate may be distributed in a manner contrary to your wishes:

- ***Spouse and parents (no children):*** In some states spouses share the estate equally with parents. In other states, the spouse may receive up to 75 percent and the parents the remaining 25 percent. An equal split between a spouse and parents, as it is in Maryland, may come as a rude surprise to many a widow or widower.

- ***Spouse and children:*** In many states, spouses inherit only half the estate. Children inherit the other half, even if they are minors. In some states, if there are two or more children, the spouse inherits only one-third of the estate and the children, even minors, inherit the remaining two-thirds.

- ***Children only:*** If there is no spouse, children inherit directly in equal portions regardless of age, special needs, or other circumstances.

- ***No known relatives:*** The state receives the entire estate.

If you have a properly drafted will, you don't need to be concerned about how your state determines the distribution of assets because the state will not decide how to divide the estate. Understanding the problems that occur without a will should motivate you to provide for loved ones through a will.

Testate—With a Will	Intestate—Without a Will
• YOU specify distribution. • YOU nominate guardian. • YOU nominate executor. • YOU can create trusts. • YOU can give to charity.	• May be costly. • LAW specifies distribution. • COURT selects guardian. • COURT selects administrator. • COURT determines special needs. • NO provision for charity.

A Christian Will

"You shall be My witnesses in Jerusalem, and in all Judea and Samaria, and to the ends of the earth" (Acts 1:8b). With these words, Jesus calls us to bear witness to the salvation that He won for all believers through His suffering and death on the cross. "But you will receive power when the Holy Spirit comes on you" (Acts 1:8a). And with this promise He enables us to serve as His witnesses through the Holy Spirit working by way of the Word.

When planning our wills, we can grow so preoccupied with how to distribute our material blessings that we may fail to share our true wealth: the Good News of forgiveness of sin and eternal life through faith in Jesus Christ. A Christian preamble to your will provides a fine opportunity to share this belief with your family and friends.

Below are two sample Christian preambles. They may be used as they are, but it may be more meaningful for you to write your own.

Preamble 1

I, _____, of the City of _____, County of _____, being of sound and disposing mind and memory and being under no restraint, do make, declare, and publish this my last Will and Testament, hereby revoking all Wills and codicils hereto made by me.

First, realizing the uncertainty of this life, I place full confidence and trust in my Lord and Savior Jesus Christ, who promised: "I am the resurrection and the life. He who believes in Me will live, even though he dies; and whosoever lives and believes in Me will never die" (John 11:25–26).

Second, knowing that the wages of sin is death, I believe that Jesus Christ, the only Son of God, suffered and died for the forgiveness of all my sins, which I neither deserve nor merit, but receive as a free gift of God, who is rich in grace and mercy.

Third, I urge my heirs not to set their hopes on uncertain riches, but to take hold of the life that is life indeed through faith in Jesus Christ. *(Then follows the body of the will.)*

Preamble 2

I, _____, of the City of _____, County of _____, and State of _____, being of sound and disposing mind and memory and being under no restraint, do make, declare and publish this my last Will and Testament, hereby revoking all Wills and codicils heretofore made by me.

First of all, I commit myself to God's care, secure in His love for me and trusting in the salvation purchased for me through Christ's suffering and death. I leave those who survive me the comfort of knowing that I have died in this faith and have joined my Lord in eternal glory.

Second, I commend my loved ones to the protecting arms of God, knowing that He will continue to provide for them despite my absence; and I encourage them to place their faith and trust in Him alone. *(Then follows the body of the will.)*[25]

Through the Holy Spirit, this personal statement of faith will comfort your loved ones in their time of loss and encourage them also to place their trust in Jesus Christ.

Gifting

We can put our love for the Lord into action with a gift through a bequest in our wills. As followers of Christ, it is fitting that our stewardship continue after death and that our estates be used wisely in God's service. Our monetary responses of thanks and love can help spread the Good News to those who follow us. There are three ways you can give through your will:

1. *Percentage:* This is the most flexible way to give. The gift automatically changes with the size of the estate (i.e., 10 percent goes to Salvation Army).

2. *Fixed amount:* This is the most common type of bequest, but not always the best. It can, of course, be changed over the years (i.e., $10,000 goes to your favorite Christian college).

3. *Residue:* This is a gift of whatever property is left after other bequests have been fulfilled (i.e., the remainder goes to World Missions).

For example, if you are married, you may want your will to state, "If my spouse does not survive me, I leave 10 percent of my estate to St. Peter's Church." You may wish to have everything go to your spouse and your gifts only be given after the death of both spouses. Your will can also specify certain assets that you want to bequest such as real estate, stocks, bonds, and collectibles.

It may be necessary for your family to continue receiving some support from your assets prior to your gifts going to charity. Many Christian denominations and other large charities will allow you to establish Charitable Remainder Trusts (see chapter 8) that can be funded at death. These Trusts provide income for up to 20 years to your dependents after which time the remaining principal of the Charitable Remainder Trusts go to charity. This arrangement is beneficial to both the family and the charity.

Choosing an Executor

In your will it is important to appoint an executor (called a personal representative in some states). To ensure that your estate is properly administered you should find someone with financial knowledge, who is organized and sensitive to the needs of your beneficiaries. Find someone who is not only competent but also willing to serve. Most states allow an executor to receive a fee based on the size of the estate. Certainly many who are selected as executors see it as an honor, but it is also hard work. The position involves many time-consuming tasks. An alternative should be identified in case the first choice is unable to do the job when the time comes. Your executor will need to:

- present the will to the appropriate courts.
- determine the need for professional help.
- pay debts and collect assets.
- notify people named as beneficiaries.
- notify social security, pension administrators, insurance companies, and financial institutions.
- manage assets, including any brokerage accounts for the estate.
- assemble and arrange for an appraisal of assets.
- compute the value of the estate.
- claim any benefits, such as life insurance or retirement accounts.
- file tax returns.
- distribute and close the estate.[26]

You can assist your executor by providing names and addresses of your professional advisors:

Accountant	_____	Insurance Agent	_____
Attorney	_____	Minister	_____
Banker	_____	Trust Officer	_____
Broker	_____	Planned Giving Counselor	_____

Location of records:

Tax records	_____	Will	_____
Safe Deposit Box	_____	Insurance Policies	_____
Investment Statements	_____		

Providing for Minors

Our children are precious gifts from God. As parents we are to provide for their well-being. In the event of the premature death of parents, minor children pose estate planning challenges. Minors can't receive or have financial assets in their names. In our absence someone will need to be responsible for raising and educating them, and nurturing their faith.

For your minor children's continued financial support, put a "minor's trust" in your will or trusts. This legal document collects, invests, and dispenses the inherited money for the benefit of the children. When the children become adults, the balance of the trust is distributed to them. The trust becomes operative on the death of both parents. Just as you manage your money for the benefit of your children during your lifetime, a minor's trust enables you to name trustees to act, after your death, as legal representatives over your assets and monies for the benefit of your children.

If there is more than one child, a decision must be made whether to have one trust for the benefit of all the children or an individual trust for each. Either way, the trust needs to specify how and when the money is to be distributed. When the children reach adulthood, it may be proper either to disperse the remaining money over several years or in one lump sum.

The selection of a guardian to raise the children in a Christian environment and a trustee for the minor's trust(s) are often difficult family choices. They may be the same person, or you may want to select separate individuals. For both the trustee and guardian selections, identify alternates in the event your first choices are unwilling or unable to accept the responsibility.

Guardian: the person responsible for your child's day-to-day well-being following your death. Specifically, the guardian of the person is responsible for your child's day-to-day care; the guardian of the estate is responsible for your child's financial well-being.

Trustee: the person or institution (e.g., a bank) you've appointed to manage the assets in a specific trust. In certain cases, it may be appropriate to name an individual and an institution as cotrustees.

149

The Estate Value

To develop an estate plan, determine what you own and calculate its value. Your asset values are determined by current fair market dollar value (the value a buyer is willing to pay). The projected gross estate value includes your house value, investments, checking accounts, vehicles, jewelry, collectibles, personal property, life insurance death proceeds, and retirement plans. Complete the following worksheet to determine your estate value.

Estate Value Ownership

Assets	Husband	Wife	Joint
Checking/bank account	$	$	$
Home	$	$	$
Stocks/bonds	$	$	$
Other investments	$	$	$
Other real estate	$	$	$
Life insurance (death benefits)	$	$	$
Retirement accounts	$	$	$
Business interests	$	$	$
Personal property	$	$	$
Other	$	$	$
Total	$	$	$

Liabilities	Husband	Wife	Joint
Mortgage	$	$	$
Consumer debt loans	$	$	$
Other	$	$	$
Total	$	$	$
Net Estate Value (assets – liabilities)	$	$	$

When death occurs, deductions are allowed for attorneys, accountants, and executor fees as well as funeral costs, probate fees, and all charitable bequests.

Federal Estate Tax

Federal estate tax is a levy on the transfer of property at death. The Federal estate tax rate is based on an individual's net estate value at death. Like income tax rates, Federal estate tax rates are progressive in nature. The more you have at death, the more you will have to pay. The following table shows the current estate tax rates:

Gift/Estate Tax Rates [27]

Taxable Estate	Estate Tax	Marginal Rate on Excess
$100,000	$23,800	0.30
150,000	38,800	0.32
250,000	70,800	0.34
500,000	155,800	0.37
750,000	248,300	0.39
1,000,000	345,800	0.41
1,250,000	448,300	0.43
1,500,000	555,800	0.45
2,000,000	780,800	0.49
2,500,000	1,025,800	0.53
3,000,000	1,290,000	0.55
10,000,000	5,140,800	0.60
21,040,000	11,764,800	0.55

The Taxpayer Relief Act of 1997 has increased the fair market value of assets exempted from gift and estate taxes as follows: 1998 ($625,000), 1999 ($650,000), 2000 and 2001 ($675,000), 2002 and 2003 ($700,000), 2004 ($850,000), 2005 and 2006 ($950,000), and thereafter ($1,000,000). This gradual increase from the past $600,000 is expected to keep pace with inflation. The exemption of $625,000 in 1998 will save approximately $200,000 in taxes. As illustrated in the table above, up to 60 percent of the estate value can be lost in taxes. If a couple has an estate in excess of $625,000, it can't be assumed that the combined husband and wife totals automatically exempt $1,250,000. For a couple to take advantage of each of their personal exemption equivalents (or unified credits), the property owned by a couple has to be divided so at the death of the first spouse that spouse's property is prevented from automatically transferring to the surviving spouse. With the current unlimited marital deduction, property at the first death normally passes to the survivor. Those with large estates need to prevent $625,000 from automatically transferring. If all the property transfers with the death of the first spouse, there will be no assets in the name of the decedent so the exemption equivalent is lost for that spouse. The surviving spouse will have the future benefits of all the assets even if they are divided.

A popular strategy to reduce the estate tax of married couples with more than $600,000 of taxable assets is to create a credit shelter trust (AB Trusts). This trust is set up so you place all or part of the $600,000 exemption equivalent into a trust and give the balance of the estate to the surviving spouse. The remaining portion may also be put into a separate trust. The credit shelter strategy accomplishes the goal of separating the estates for tax purposes.

If your personal estate has in excess of $1,250,000 and you do no planning, approximately $240,000 will be lost in taxes (see Gift/Estate Tax Rates table). To spend approximately two thousand dollars on attorney fees to draft a trust would be very beneficial. Many of us will not have estates above $625,000 so tax planning will not be necessary.

In addition to federal estate taxes, most states impose state death taxes. Although less severe, more of us will be affected by state taxes than the federal taxes because federal law allows the unified credit which exempts up to $625,000 of property from federal taxes. You will pay taxes in the state where you have your residence at death.

If you own real estate in more than one state, you may owe taxes in each of those states. The following table shows the current maximum tax rates, some of which may affect your individual estate plan.

Income tax (retirement plans)	15%–39.6%
Gift taxes	55%–60%
Estate taxes	55%–60%
Generation skipping tax	55%
State death tax	5%–10% (est.)

Annual Gift Tax Exclusion

This exclusion allows you the opportunity to give to another person $10,000 per year without reducing your exemption equivalent. In any year, if you exceed the $10,000 per individual, you must file a gift tax form that reduces the $625,000 exemption equivalent for use at a later date. Husbands and wives may jointly make a gift to the same child or some other individual, which allows a gift

152

of $20,000 to that person. (After 1998, the Taxpayer Relief Act of 1997 will index to inflation the $10,000 annual gift tax exclusion.)

The ability to give away a limited amount of money without any tax liability is a big tax break for wealthy families. In addition to the tax break advantage, giving money away during your lifetime allows you the enjoyment of watching someone else enjoy your gift.

Durable Power of Attorney

A durable power of attorney is a written instrument with which one person, the principal, authorizes another, the attorney-in-fact, to act for him or her. It is durable, meaning it continues even if the principal becomes incompetent. The designated agent can handle an individual's legal and financial affairs in the event an accident or health problem causes the person to be unable to handle them. A durable power of attorney is one of the safest, simplest, and cheapest ways of continuing the management of your affairs in the event of incapacity. By not having a durable power of attorney, a court would need to appoint a conservator. These probate court proceedings can be costly and time-consuming.

A durable power of attorney is effective only while the principal is alive, but it can specify estate planning actions to be taken if the client becomes disabled. One action among many would be to continue or begin a charitable gifting strategy. It may also be used to give someone the right to place property into revocable living trusts. Your durable power of attorney may be as broad or narrow in powers as you wish. You may authorize the individual whom you select to manage your financial affairs (attorney-in-fact) to virtually handle all financial matters or you may be very specific about what you want the person to handle. The selection of an attorney-in-fact or agent needs to be done with care because that person may be given authority to collect, invest, and disperse money. If a professional is used, fees may be involved.

Living Will and Health Care Directives

A living will sets out your wishes about how life-prolonging treatment should be provided or withheld if you become unable to communicate those wishes for yourself. A living will tells your family and doctors what you would like to have done in certain medical situations. Because of the 1991 Patient Self-Determination Act, you are forced to discuss living wills should you be admitted to a hospital. Living wills can be drawn up by lawyers or by some doctors' offices.

As is the case with a Durable Power of Attorney, you write your Living Will when you are competent and of sound mind. In conjunction with your Living Will you should also complete a document called a Durable Power of Attorney for Health Care. With this instrument you designate the person (typically your spouse) whom you want to make health care decisions on your behalf in the event you are not able to make these decisions yourself. You can revoke this authority at any time.

Revocable Living Trusts

A trust is a written legal document that transfers assets to a trustee. The trustee received legal title to the property placed in the trust and manages assets according to the living trust. The person establishing the trust is called the grantor or settlor. (The grantor or settlor may be the trustee.) The trustee manages the property for the benefit of the third person, who is called the beneficiary. (The grantor may also be the beneficiary.)

The revocable living trust is "revocable" because it can be altered or revised at any time. It is a "living" trust because it is created during the lifetime of the grantor or settlor. Revocable living trusts are created so that the assets are transferred to the trustee during his or her lifetime. This lifetime transfer is a great advantage for the grantor of the trust because if the grantor becomes unable to manage his assets, the trustee can manage the estate on his behalf.

The advantages of revocable living trusts over wills are considerable. Under a will, an estate must be settled in probate court resulting in lawyer's fees and court fees. In contrast, a revocable living trust is settled without a court proceeding. A successor trustee simply distributes assets according to the trust instructions. Bypassing probate will save a considerable amount of money and the estate will be settled more quickly. Because revocable living trusts avoid probate, they do not become public record, so the transferring of assets with living trusts maintains confidentiality.

Contesting a revocable living trust is more difficult than contesting a will. During the will probate process, the court asks those with a claim against the estate to come forward, which can be done without an attorney. Any disgruntled party against a trust would need an attorney.

There are a few disadvantages of revocable living trusts. For a revocable living trust to function, all assets with a title need to be put in the name of the trust. It is an inconvenience, but you must transfer the titles of homes, bank accounts, brokerage accounts, businesses, and other investments into the name of the trust. A second disadvantage is that the expense of setting up a revocable living trust is much greater than that to set up a will.

Pour-Over Wills

A pour-over will is used in conjunction with a revocable living trust. It is likely that, when setting up a trust, either intentionally or accidentally, there are assets that were not put in the name of the trust. If the property title is not in the name of the trust or the trust does not refer to an asset, the trust cannot accept that property. The pour-over will acts as a catch-all and directs everything that was not properly titled in the trust to the trust, but it must first go through probate. The pour-over will is a back-up security measure to ensure everything is properly transferred.

Selecting a Trustee

Trustees for a revocable living trust may be individuals or entities such as banks or trust companies. Many people feel the best trustee is a trusted friend or family member because he or she is more likely to act on behalf of the grantor and for the benefit of the beneficiary. It is also helpful if the person is knowledgeable in financial affairs.

The drawback to the choice of one individual as opposed to an organization is his or her willingness and ability to serve. A trustee has legal liabilities and responsibilities that many individuals may not want to assume or be able to fulfill satisfactorily. Corporate trustees, as opposed to individuals, are well-equipped to serve in the trustee capacity. Corporate trustees offer these advantages:

- experience in estate matters
- investment expertise
- accounting and recordkeeping ability
- safekeeping of assets
- willingness and ability to serve
- objectivity
- less incidence of integrity criticisms

The disadvantages of corporate trustees are the fees and the possible lack of personal attention.

Common Estate Planning Mistakes

Many mistakes can be made when you are planning for the distribution of your estate. Some of the most common errors include:

1. *Not writing a will.* In the event a deceased person does not have a will, his or her assets are distributed according to state intestacy statutes. What the surviving family members receive is determined by the state. Without a will you lose control of your estate, the expense of administering it increases, and the inheritance to your heirs decreases.

2. *Failure to update a will.* After a will is drafted, don't just put it away in a safe place and forget about it. As family and financial circumstances change, your will should be updated. Review your will every two or three years to determine if any changes are needed.

3. *Sloppy or poor recordkeeping.* Make a detailed list of your assets with account numbers, the location of insurance policies and important papers. Your list should include names and addresses of any financial advisors as well.

4. *Simple will.* A simple will is the most basic will where everything is left to a surviving spouse. This could result in higher taxes upon the death of the second spouse. For estates over $625,000, both spouses should take advantage of their own unified credit.

5. *Failure to monitor estate growth.* Estate values often increase so your planning should allow for that. If your estate is now below $625,000, with inflation, savings programs, and good investments, your estate can easily grow to exceed that amount. Plan accordingly.

6. *Estate valuation.* Often estate values are underestimated because you may not be aware of what is included. Remember that life insurance death benefits, personal property, and retirement plans are all part of estate values.

7. *Lack of liquidity.* Estates may be substantial but have assets that are not liquid. This could cause a problem when cash is needed to pay estate taxes. Life insurance may be purchased to provide the estate liquidity.

8. *No plan to transfer business.* It is not uncommon for business owners to lack a plan for continued operation of the business upon their death. A proper plan is necessary for an orderly succession of the business. Little or no planning can cause a much greater tax burden.

9. *Poor choice of executor.* The executor position is often a time-consuming one. Many individuals who are chosen are not able or willing to give the time necessary. When selecting an executor, look both at his or her competence and willingness to serve.[28]

Everyone will have an estate plan at death. You can write your own, or you can allow your state of residence to make it for you. The Christian estate plan you write is the only one that will distribute the assets you've accumulated over a lifetime the way you want them distributed.

If you haven't prepared an estate plan, now is the time to do it—even if you don't have a large estate. Gather information, make plans, and set up an appointment with an attorney to review them. Communicate your desires to your family, uncomfortable as it may be to discuss these things. Remember that your last will and testament is your last opportunity to share your love for the Lord with your friends and family—it is a document that can share your faith and demonstrate your faithful stewardship: "Be faithful, even to the point of death, and I will give you the crown of life" (Revelation 2:10).

Questions for Personal Reflection

Use the following questions to help you focus on your understanding of estate planning.

Faithful and responsible management of God's money continues through Christian estate planning. It's easy to get caught up in the idea that a will deals only with property, but it actually deals with people. It is important that a will provide for the disbursement of tangible assets but it can also be a statement of Christian faith.

1. What does 1 Timothy 5:8 say about our need to provide for our families?

2. What is more important to leave to our children than our material possessions?

3. Do even small estates need a will? Why or why not?

4. How can a will be beneficial in saving administrative expenses and time?

5. What does it mean to give a residual gift? a percentage gift? a fixed amount?

6. What human emotions will work against our need to give (Luke 12:15; Colossians 3:5)?

7. What tax benefits do we receive from our charitable gifting in our wills?

8. For tax purposes, are some assets better to give than others? Why?

9. Who benefits from our generosity (Philippians 4:17)?

10. What size of estate do we need to have to be liable for Federal estate taxes?

11. What are some ways to reduce or eliminate tax liabilities?

12. For whom would a revocable living trust be appropriate?

Endnotes

[1]Carl W. Berner Sr., *The Power of Pure Stewardship* (St. Louis, Missouri: Concordia Publishing House, 1970) 33.

[2]*Men's Manual*, volume II (Oak Brook, Illinois: Institute in Basic Life Principles, Inc., 1983) 22–25.

[3]Warren Arndt (Speaker), *ABC's of Stewardship* (Sermon Audio Tapes) Faith Lutheran Church, Troy, Michigan, 1996.

[4]Arthur E. Graf, *The Church in the Community: An Effective Evangelism Program for the Christian Congregation* (Grand Rapids, Michigan: Wm. B. Eerdmans Publishing Co., 1965) 13. Used by permission of the publisher.

[5]Randy C. Alcorn, *Money, Possessions and Eternity* (Wheaton, Illinois: Tyndale House Publishers, Inc., 1989) 205. Used by permission of Tyndale House Publishers, Inc. All rights reserved.

[6]T.K. Thompson, *Stewardship Illustrations* (Englewood Cliffs, New Jersey: Prentice Hall, 1965) 15.

[7]Ibid. 10.

[8]Glenn Van Ekeren, *Speaker's Sourcebook II* (Englewood Cliffs, New Jersey: Prentice Hall, 1993) 171. Used by permission of Prentice Hall/Career & Personal Development.

[9]Ibid. 12.

[10]Ibid. 12.

[11]Paul Chiles and Dr. Dennis R. Kaz, *A Guide for Financial Freedom* (self-published, 1993) 27.

[12]Charles F. Stanley (Speaker), *Financial Wisdom* (Audio Tape Series) (Atlanta, Georgia: In Touch Ministries, 1996).

[13]Ibid.

[14]Ibid.

[15]Robert J. Garner, Robert B. Coplan, Barbara J. Raasch, and Charles L. Ratner, *Ernst and Young's Personal Financial Planning Guide* (New York, New York: John Wiley & Sons, Inc., 1995) 53.

[16]Larry Chambers and Kenn Miller, *The First Time Investor* (Chicago, Illinois: Probus Publishing Company, 1994) 57–58.

[17]Ibid. 133.

[18]Ibid. 41.

[19]Ethan Pope, *How to Be a Smart Money Manager* (Nashville, Tennessee: Thomas Nelson, Inc., 1995) 158.

[20]Larry Burkett, *Using Your Money Wisely* (Chicago, Illinois: Moody Press, 1985) 140–142.

[21]Larry Burkett, *Preparing for Retirement* (Chicago, Illinois: Moody Press, 1992) 68.

[22]Anne Willette, "Women Need to Save More Money than Men Do," *USA Today*, 29 May 1996.

[23]Frank Logan, "Philosophy of Planned Giving," (First of a Three-Part Sermon Series, 1996) 1–2.

[24]Scott C. Fithian, *Social Capital: From Success to Significance* (Boston, Massachusetts: Legacy Advisory Associates, Inc., 1995) viii–4.

25"You Can Plant Love Harvest Forever through a Christian Will." The Lutheran Church—Missouri Synod Foundation, St. Louis, Missouri. (*Note:* These preambles are provided as samples. Check with your own church body to see if similar preambles are available. Or write your own, expressing your faith.)

[26]*Estate Planning Concepts*, 7th Edition (Indianapolis, Indiana: Pictorial, 1990) 38.

[27]Ibid. 105.

[28]Barbara O'Neill, *Saving on a Shoestring* (Chicago, Illinois: Dearborn Financial Publishing, Inc., 1995) 190–192.